SCREEN SKILLS

ABOUT THE AUTHORS

Roger Wooster (M.A. (Distinction), PGCE, BA (Hons)) has worked in theatre, radio and television during his career. He went on to work in FE and HE (including the Newport Film School), teaching a wide range of performing arts modules including screen and radio acting. During his career he has had the opportunity to observe the different styles of Mike Leigh and Ken Russell at work. He has given papers at many international conferences and has been widely published in a range of academic journals. His *Contemporary Theatre in Education* was published in 2006 and in 2016 a major study of educational theatre, *Theatre in Education in Britain*, was published by Methuen Drama.

Paul Conway (PGCE, Diploma in Speech and Drama, Brendan Smith Theatre Academy, Dublin) has spent his career working in film, television, stage and radio as an actor, director, devisor and published playwright. As a young actor he worked on the TV series *Inside* and was writer-director of *The Last Shout* for Sahara Films. He has also worked for directors such as Ken Loach, Ken Russell, Desmond Davis and Gerald Stembridge. Since moving into academia he has specialised in teaching screen performance. He is currently Senior Lecturer at the Film and Television School based at the University of South Wales, Cardiff.

SCREEN ACTING SKILLS

A Practical Handbook for Students and Tutors

Roger Wooster and Paul Conway

methuen | drama
LONDON • NEW YORK • OXFORD • NEW DELHI • SYDNEY

METHUEN DRAMA
Bloomsbury Publishing Plc
50 Bedford Square, London, WC1B 3DP, UK
1385 Broadway, New York, NY 10018, USA

BLOOMSBURY, METHUEN DRAMA and the Methuen Drama logo are trademarks of Bloomsbury Publishing Plc

First published in Great Britain 2020

Cover design: Charlotte Daniels
Cover image © Abby Timms

A catalogue record for this book is available from the British Library.

Library of Congress Cataloging-in-Publication Data
Names: Wooster, Roger, author. | Conway, Paul (Dramatist), author.
Title: Screen acting skills: a practical handbook for students and tutors/ Roger Wooster and Paul Conway.
Description: London, UK; New York, NY: Methuen Drama/Bloomsbury Publishing Plc, 2020. | Includes bibliographical references.
Identifiers: LCCN 2019012538| ISBN 9781350093041 (hbk.) | ISBN 9781350093034 (pbk.) | ISBN 9781350093072 (xml platform) | ISBN 9781350093058 (ePDF) | ISBN 9781350093065 (ebk.)
Subjects: LCSH: Motion picture acting–Study and teaching.
Classification: LCC PN1995.9.A26 W66 2020 | DDC 791.4302/8–dc23 LC record available at https://lccn.loc.gov/2019012538

ISBN: HB: 978-1-3500-9304-1
PB: 978-1-3500-9303-4
ePDF: 978-1-3500-9305-8
eBook: 978-1-3500-9306-5

Typeset by Integra Software Services Pvt. Ltd.

To find out more about our authors and books visit www.bloomsbury.com and sign up for our newsletters.

Thanks to Anita, Lily and Bella for endless teas and to Emily, Eirlys and Blake for being there.

Also to all our students, past and present, who contributed to the development of the ideas contained in this book.

CONTENTS

FIGURES

WEBSITE EXERCISES

The following exercises are available via the website: https://vimeo.com/channels/1445243v

In the examples given, students are trying out the exercises for the first time. Discuss with your groups the strengths and weaknesses and how they can learn from them to improve their own approaches.

Exercise	2:3	What do you mean?
Exercise	3:2	Say again?
Exercise	4:2	Hook up, make up, break up
Exercise	4:3	Look at me when you're ignoring me!
Exercise	5:1	The confrontation
Exercise	5:2	The letter
Exercise	6:2	Scary and Shouty
Exercise	6:3	The corpse at the funeral
Exercise	7:2	Are you listening? Really listening?
Exercise	7:4	Mini-dialogues
Exercise	7:5	Did I hear you right?
Exercise	8:3	Time warp
Exercise	9:1	Cheating positions: you're sitting on my lap
Exercise	9:2	On your marks: getting to the right place and staying there
Exercise	9:6	Look at me and say that
Exercise	10:4	Pick a genre, any genre
Exercise	11:1	I'm on the phone
Exercise	11:2	Next! Setting up a mock audition
Exercise	12:3	Speak *and* act?
Exercise	12:4	I wasn't expecting that!

ACKNOWLEDGEMENTS

We would like to express our thanks to Equity UK for permission to reproduce the text from their 'Creating Safe Spaces' card. Also to the actors who have offered up the advice and anecdotes which we have fed into these pages: Philip Bird, Debbie Bridge, Alan David, Mark Gowers, John Halstead, Tom Hardman, Sophie Houston, Ava Hunt, Robert Kirwan, Richard Knight, Sarah Leigh and Maria Palios-Potts.

The chapter on auditions was greatly enhanced by the contributions from Judith Gay at Edward Wyman Casting, Debi Maclean from Regan Management, Nicola Reynolds Casting and by the actor Tom Mumford.

Thanks are also due to the technicians at the University of South Wales, and Anita Reynolds for their help in documenting the exercises for both the book and its accompanying website material, to Simon Hyland for the diagrams, to Luigi Caramella for Figures 2 and 11 and to Abby Timms for the rest of the photography. For their generous participation, thanks are due to students and graduates of the University of South Wales: Panayia Argyridou, Nerida Bradley, Aneta Brasnickova, Luigi Caramella, Imran Chaudhry, Lucie-Anne Davies, Lauren Ensor, Shannon Gilley, Gavin Jones, Stan Kirby, James Lawrence, Shannon Lee, Stacey Mallon, Rachel Mann, Robert J. Mason, Imogen Powell, Pasher Prazsky, Lili Reynolds, Nadia Souffi, James Spiller, Olli Veteläinen, Devante Williams-Fleming – with apologies that not all appear in the final edit. Thanks to Viv Mainwaring for his advice on the technical glossary and to Alison Steadman for reading the first draft and giving such positive feedback.

We are also grateful to the Donat family and Manchester University for making available to readers the ground-breaking 'Emotion Chart' devised by the film actor Robert Donat in 1938. Thanks especially to Dr Victoria Lowe and Stella Halkyard for making this possible.

And many thanks to Eirlys for lending her first shoes.

INTRODUCTION: READY FOR 'ACTION!'

This book offers students and tutors a compendium of exercises that will help develop screen acting skills alongside some general information about what to expect during a film shoot. By 'students' we mean those studying screen acting but we also include young actors, and older actors new to screen performance. By 'tutors' we mean to include those teaching screen acting in schools, colleges and universities but also workshop leaders in any learning environment. Aspiring directors may also find the book useful for the insights it offers into the way actors work. We encourage you to use this book as a resource: a source of information about what actually happens during a shoot and how to tailor acting skills to the needs of the screen. We invite you to either 'dip in' to the chapters to address key acting issues or to use the book as framework for curriculum work.

For students and anyone new to screen acting, the first section of each chapter presents information about certain aspects of performance to camera and includes both advice on the skills required and what to expect from life as a professional screen actor. Much of your acting experience will probably have been based in theatrical traditions and you will have to learn how to adjust these to the small or large screen. Whilst the skills you have learned will be a solid foundation for your screen work, there are going to be significant differences in approach, in delivery, in procedures and protocols. We hope you will find the information in these narrative sections of each chapter a useful context for the practical exercises that you undertake with a workshop leader. A few of them you may be able to tackle in the privacy of your own space, and some of them you could undertake with colleagues in a study group situation using whatever level of technical equipment you have at your disposal. We do not generally recommend working without camera and playback facilities, for it is only on screen that you will see the true value of your work. It is important to analyse the screen – not the live – performance.

For workshop leaders the narratives which form the first section of the chapters will serve as a context in which they can help actors develop their skills through the employment of the range of practical exercises that follow. These vary a great deal, some involving short improvisations, some using short sections of text which can be learned on the spot and others for which it will be necessary to allow students time to prepare. Most of these games are original (as far as we know), whilst others have been adapted over the years from the canon of theatre training that we here adapt to new purposes. Some require little or no text, for we must constantly remind ourselves that film is essentially a visual medium. It would be a brave piece of avant-garde theatre that ran for two and a half hours with no dialogue in the first and last twenty minutes, as is the case with *2001: A Space Odyssey* (Stanley Kubrick, 1968). Or consider the film *127 Hours* (Danny Boyle, 2010), whose dialogue comprises a very small part of the eighty-eight pages of the total screenplay and an even smaller part of the actual running time. The visual components and the art direction of movies contributes at least as much to their success as the quality of the screen acting to which they provide the backdrop.

Each chapter focuses on a particular screen acting skill, though it will soon become clear that the exercises, and the skills they seek to nurture, will have multiple applications and, as the student becomes more adept, will reinforce previous skills whilst offering the challenge of new ones. Indeed, there is a danger of suggesting that screen acting is just a matter of mastering a series of techniques, ticking the boxes, and then finding success. Ultimately, of course, the success comes from the way that the individual actor's talent and insight meld the skills together with coherence. Opportunities for this are offered in **Chapter 10: Finding the art of You** – where exercises include ideas for short films in which talents, skills and studio know-how can be brought together.

We recognize that the availability of technology and technical support will vary enormously from institution to institution and from situation to situation. Most students have a camera in their pocket and virtually all educational establishments will have a suitable viewing screen of some order. But this book is about the acting and we have tried to make all the exercises achievable with the minimum of resources. We recommend that the studio or workshop space be set out in such a way that those undertaking the exercise can be observed in real time and then critically reviewed by the group. The observers should watch the screen and not the live action for it is the screen performance that they are there to consider. A suggested basic studio arrangement is set out in Figure 1. Of course, many universities, colleges and film schools may have an army of technicians, multiple cameras, editing suites and post-production facilities and these can be used to develop the scale of many of the exercises. For the aspiring screen actor though, the basic skills required can be practised with the minimum of technical paraphernalia. A camera, a projector, a screen; these are the tools that the screen actor needs in order to learn, develop and share her art.

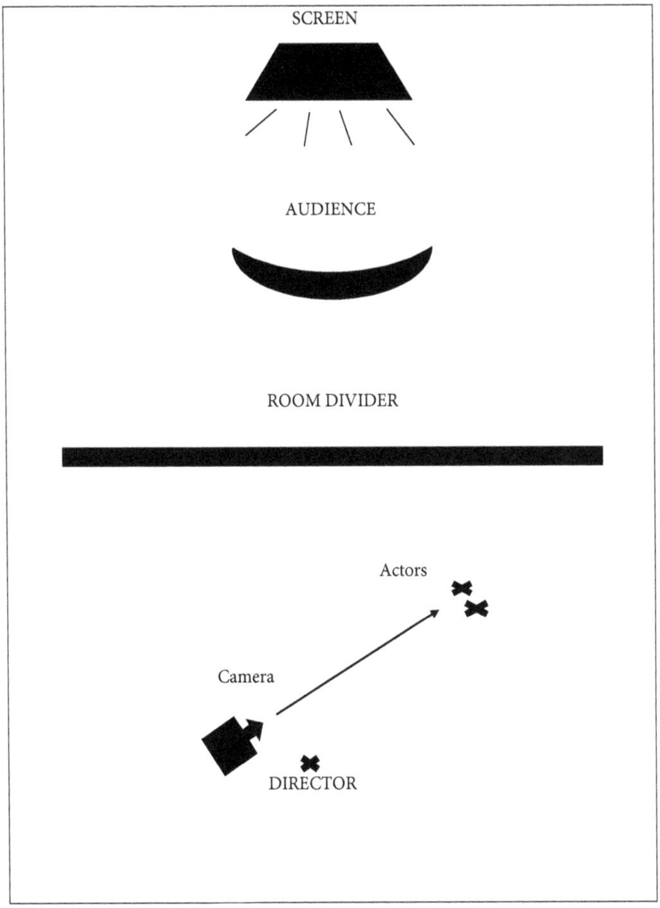

FIGURE 1 Suggested basic layout for studio exercises. Courtesy of Simon Hyland.

Coping with larger groups can be a major challenge for tutors and workshop leaders in some teaching situations. Students want to be up there, in front of the camera honing their skills. Frustration can set in quickly if one spends all one's time watching the efforts of others. Generally, we would recommend that when facing such pressures, individual exposure to each exercise is kept brief with minimal discussion until extracts from all the contributions are reviewed. However, we regard thorough, honest and supportive discussion to be a central part of the learning process. Feedback and analysis should not become a beauty contest: 'that is better than that'. All contributions should be recognized for the effort that has gone into them; there is rarely, if ever, a definitive 'perfect' performance. Further, it is good practice from the outset to impose studio discipline during these recordings. Get into the habit of insisting on 'Quiet on the set!' before each recording. Audience reaction (and analysis) can be liberated when the footage is reviewed. Other strategies for large numbers might include the use of multiple cameras (even phone cameras), with students working in groups around the room or rooms, and then allowing a short period of studio silence for each to record their work prior to a group sharing. It may also be possible to prepare work outside the confines of the timetabled lesson. Different exercises will present different problems, but with care and careful strategies tutors can keep all students engaged.

Seeing yourself on screen can be traumatic (as we will discuss in later chapters) and all groups must be reminded of the need to be caring and supportive. An environment of mutual respect and developmental feedback needs to be established from the outset. Many professional actors avoid watching themselves on screen. Johnny Depp, in an interview with Rob Blackwelder in 1999, declared that he avoids watching his own movies:

> I condition myself to believe that once the scene is done, once the movie is done, my job is done, and whatever happens after that is none of my business.[1]

We believe, though, that an atmosphere of mutual support and positive criticism is not only good for the student but also maximizes the time-saving value of learning from others' experiences. As actors, our 'selves' are

[1]Rob Blackwelder, 'Deppth Perception', splicedwire.com, 12 November 1999. Available at: http://splicedwire.com/features/depp.html [accessed 20 May 2019].

the canvas of our art and displaying it in public requires the courage to expose our vulnerability. That is why criticism hurts so much – whether in a local paper review or from our co-workers. We need to have very thick skins at times, for criticism can seem to be aimed not just at our work but at our very souls as artists. Our bodies and our thought processes, our words and our reactions, are the media of our art, and we have to accept this exposure, both physical and mental. We have to let go of our hang-ups – ego and self-image can be our enemies. The workshop floor is the place where we can learn to let go of these fears. This requires an atmosphere of trust to which you, the student, must contribute. It is important to be part of a working environment where criticism can be given and taken without tears. 'That was awful, I didn't believe that at all!' may be true but it is not a useful comment. Rather, both workshop leader and fellow student should perhaps invite the actor to comment first – can she or he see any problems? Then allow others to come in: 'I think it might have worked better if you kept avoiding his glance when you said that.' 'Why?' 'Well, it would help us to understand why the character felt that … ' And so on. We need to offer maximum support (especially when the members of the group are new to each other) to prevent actors becoming defensive of their work and self-censoring of their creativity. Failure to do this can lead to denial: 'I don't see the problem!', or lack of confidence: 'I don't want to look' or even 'I may as well give up then!' Developing positive ways of giving and receiving criticism is an invaluable skill to take forward into what can be a very challenging and combative career.

We have assumed that most students and tutors/workshop leaders coming to this book will be familiar with acting terms such as 'emotion memory' derived from theatre and especially from the ideas and influence of Constantin Stanislavski. In this book we freely use Stanislavskian terms such as 'objectives', 'previous circumstances' and 'motivation' as we take our readers through the games and exercises. A brief explanation is inserted on the first use of such terms and a complete glossary of these explanations is included at the end of the book. A separate glossary also lists brief definitions of some of the technical jargon that will be heard on the studio floor and which, again, we occasionally make use of in this book.

To augment the points we raise, we have offered some quotations from well-known actors and directors and also invited contemporary actors to recount their early experiences of being on a shoot. We offer links to clips from films to illustrate points we are trying to make, which can be accessed online. Blockbuster films come and go, and so, despite the latest multimillion-dollar extravaganza being at the forefront of many young actors' minds, we have tended to take examples from films which seem to be withstanding the tests of time and which rely on acting and character exploration rather than on action and chaotic explosions. The keen film-acting student will quickly develop their own instincts and preferences, and no doubt workshop leaders too will have their own favourites and pet hates.

Our approach to the development of screen acting skills

Most will be familiar with the term 'Method Acting' or 'The Method' espoused by such actors as James Dean, Marlon Brando, Marilyn Monroe, Robert De Niro, Heath Ledger, Daniel Day-Lewis, Angelina Jolie, Tom Hanks, Anne Hathaway, Dustin Hoffman – the list is endless. 'The Method', of course, is shorthand for 'the Stanislavski Method' from where most acting – and especially screen acting – today has evolved. It remains a foundation stone of most acting techniques favoured on stage and screen. Stanislavski's ideas have been further evolved by such trainers and directors as Lee Strasberg (who encouraged actors to use their own experience to help them identify with their character), Stella Adler (who put greater emphasis on the use of the imagination and research) and Sanford Meisner (who required his actors to focus completely on the actor with whom they are working to the exclusion of all else). Tutors and student actors will find ways of accessing all these Stanislavski-derived approaches through many of the exercises in this book, but we have tried to avoid such artistic schisms; what we seek to offer is a sound generic approach to the various challenges thrown at us by screen acting roles. Those interested in the specialized acting philosophies of those name above will find suggestion for further reading in the 'recommended further reading' section of the bibliography.

In **Chapter 1: Don't act, *be!*** we consider how acting for film has evolved. Early silent films drew heavily on stylized theatrical techniques, which are also evident in early sound movies. As technologies of sound, lighting and recording developed, along with appropriate screenwriting techniques, acting, too, evolved into the naturalistic style that predominates today. Other acting styles are possible and may come into vogue in the future, but even (for example) today's fantasy and sci-fi movies rely heavily on psychologies, motivations and objectives based on our own memes of living. Even within the accepted contemporary acting style, there are films that strain towards heightened realism – Wes Anderson's *The Grand Budapest Hotel* (2014) and Martin Scorsese's *Hugo* (2011), for example.

This chapter also considers the differences in approach between acting on stage and acting for the camera: in the theatre the audience's eye can roam freely and choices made by the actor will affect where it decides to settle, whilst on screen the camera makes the decision; the power of the actor's fearful stare may be lost, since the camera has chosen to settle instead upon the nervous tapping foot. Acting techniques also vary depending upon the genre. Drama, romcom, sitcom, soap opera, procedural police drama, forensics drama, hospital drama – all require different approaches in the delivery and timing of lines. Each film or TV series will have a 'house style' that will be maintained by the writing team and the director.

There are two foundation stones of acting (in any medium) that crop up frequently throughout the book. The first is the need to *listen* to the other actors, and the second is the necessity of establishing a coherent *backstory* to determine all aspects of your character's behaviour, appearance and motivations. In **Chapter 2: Backchat**, we offer some straightforward approaches to creating your character's present by building an understanding of their past. The clues come from the script and from your own research and imagination but, unlike theatre, less from rehearsal and direction. Whether your character is an alien life form that was born in a hatchery, or Attila the Hun or Bigfoot, you will have to discover or invent a backstory so that you can navigate the present of the screen performance.

Chapter 3 encourages you to consider **The actor as plumber** – well, any contractor will do! We recommend the putting aside of ego and the recognition that (at least until you are a megastar) actors are there to serve the whim of the director. You are there to do a job. You come prepared, you behave professionally and you hope to get more (and more challenging) work in the future. This is perhaps what Depp is referring to in his comments quoted above. This chapter also contains some advice about coping with being on a set together for the first time, including some dos and don'ts. The exercises offered here are generic and seek to focus and calm the actor, whilst alerting them to the possibilities that, with the help of that backstory, there are more ways of approaching a text than the obvious!

In **Chapter 4** we get into specifics. The suggestions in this chapter are no more or less important than any others, but we have to start somewhere and we chose to start with **Keeping it real**. You may choose to start with other chapters and with other exercises, and that's fine. In this chapter we consider the importance of concentration and how this differs from the concentration required of the stage actor. The actor on screen may have to work with far more distractions in the shape of perhaps dozens of people also doing their jobs and apparently ignoring your masterful performance. The chronology of performance will probably be absent (something we discuss more fully in Chapter 8), with scenes being shot out of sequence, in different locations and with no personal control over which take the director and editor will use. High levels of concentration are required, not least on the other actors, so that you can respond to them appropriately in each take. Listening (truly *listening*, not just waiting for your cue) is central to all the work the screen actor does.

In life we rarely know exactly what is going to happen next. Even if we know the general, we certainly don't know the specific. **Chapter 5** is entitled **This has never happened to me before**. No it hasn't, not even on the twelfth take. The exercises here are about not anticipating your lines, the lines of others and even your own emotions. It doesn't happen until it happens and the screen actor must develop the skill of living in the moment. Being natural takes practice, and undertaking the exercises provided here and reviewing them with supportive peers will help develop the necessary skills. In this chapter we use a good deal of improvisational work as, in improv, we truly have to react to the unexpected at every turn. We need to be alive to what our fellow actors are bringing to the performance, to respond to the circumstances of the situation, and to respond to the needs of the director even when we disagree with them!

Chapter 6: Where am I? *When* am I? builds on notions of backstory. If you just beam down onto the set, in a daze, wondering what's going on, staring at all the techie kit, wondering why it takes so many miles of cable, being caught in the blinding lights whilst what appears to be a furry mammal is suspended over your head, you are not going to give a good performance. Instead, you have to be able to create the belief in the world of the film – the underground lair, the high-powered office, the laboratory, the car, the prison escape tunnel, the bank vault. And in one of the most challenging environments, the actor may be required to perform in a completely neutral environment – against a green screen – which will then be magically transformed by the techno-wizards into a raging sea, a crumbling clifftop or hoards of aliens emerging from their intergalactic space transporter. The screen actor has to have the imagination to realize (in both senses of the word) where she is and make it real for us.

Are you listening to me? Let's face it, we all have an 'egosystem' and part of wanting to be an actor is to be told that we are good at it. We put our very bodies and voices up there on the screen for others to enjoy (we hope) and we *will* be judged. That takes guts and not a small measure of ego. We have to believe that what we have to offer is worth others watching. For us, listening is the key. **Chapter 7: Are you listening to me?** offers a range of exercises to hone this skill. Having listened, we can then respond within the context of all we know about our own character and the circumstances surrounding the situation. So listening becomes about relating to the other person and truthfully responding to what we have received from them. The exercises in this chapter are about being generous as a performer: giving out energy rather than sucking it in. It is about making those around you look good – your fellow actors and all the creative technical team. It is about trusting your fellow performers and the technical roles working alongside you. Picking up on ideas in earlier chapters, the exercises offer practice in responding truthfully to what fellow actors are bringing forward: interpretations of text, the use of props and the exploration and exploitation of situations. Despite the lingering presence of that nagging ego, we encourage actors to be humble on the shoot: to show us you're interesting and not tell us you're interesting.

> Listening is not merely hearing. Listening is reacting. Listening is being affected by what you hear. Listening is active (Michael Shurtleff).[2]

In **Chapters 8 and 9** we explore in more detail the technical requirements within which your acting skills need to flourish. In **Where were we?** we consider the problems that can arise during a recording process which may be neither chronological – nor even *logical*! It can often happen that for reasons beyond the director's control a shoot has to be interrupted. Maybe the crew is in danger of going into expensive overtime, there is a technical

---

[2]Quoted on AZQuotes.com. Available at: https://www.azquotes.com/author/21779-Michael_Shurtleff [accessed 25 July 2018].

hitch or the light has become unworkable. It may in these circumstances be necessary to return to the shoot hours, days – even months – later. Or it may be necessary to shoot the end of the emotionally highly charged argument in the street *now* – whilst the extras are around – and only then move to the apartment to see the argument begin and develop. This second shoot might even take place weeks later. How can one map not only the continuity of appearance but also, crucially, emotional pitch? This chapter offers exercises where the students can learn to develop these skills.

In our exploration of skills and techniques we have thrown in a good deal about the technical protocols of working on a shoot. In **Chapter 9** we turn our attention firmly to the technical demands made of the actors and which they must keep in mind whilst dazzling us with the quality of their actual acting. **It's good to cheat** lays out some of the requirements beyond performance that actors have to deal with in order to help the director achieve what she is aiming for. 'Cheating' is the industry jargon for those occasions when it is necessary to bend the spatial and performance rules so that it looks 'right' on screen. In this chapter you will find information and exercises on cheating positions, eyelines, vocal level and finding your position when walking into shot ('finding your mark'). The screen actor has to be able to use such artifices in order to hide them successfully, for the only truth will be what appears on screen. This will involve submitting to the wisdom of the director and his team; what feels right may not look right, and somehow you have to maintain your truthful performance amongst this melee of deceit.

So, the bulk of this book is about considering the necessary screen acting skills as 'bite-sized' chunks of expertise and technical knowledge, but eventually these have to be assembled into a coherent performance. **Chapter 10: Finding the art of You** suggests ways of doing this primarily through the creation of short films. Even these filmmaking exercises can be undertaken with minimal technology – for some of them even a single unedited take could suffice. In institutions with more time and resources, they can of course be developed into short, edited film productions with all the post-production paraphernalia. These exercises can also be used for assessment purposes if part of a screen acting curriculum. What we are seeking to offer in this chapter is a means by which your own talent can be fused and enhanced with competency in the skills outlined in earlier chapters. Though not the primary aim of this book, the exercises in Chapter 10 might also offer opportunities for the creation of showreels for audition purposes.

Chapter 11: Audition peace offers some general advice on preparing for auditions. You may think that success is just about the audition and be tempted to skip straight to this chapter. We hope not, because the suggestions in Chapter 11 are very much built upon the training and techniques discussed and practised in the earlier chapters. In writing this chapter, we have talked to young working actors, agents and casting directors and we make some suggestions on how to approach auditions and offer some dos and don'ts that may increase your chances. We discuss skills and further training as well as how to cope with both the inevitable rejection and the possibility of success.

It's a WRAP! Well, just about. In this final chapter we consider a few of the things that have sort of got missed along the way. A few more words about auditions and your appearance, and we also raise the issue of the acting approaches required for different genres, especially comedy, and what to expect when working with directors and their differing methods. In this chapter we also advise on the sensitive issue of dealing with roles that require intimacy and possibly even nudity and the importance of protecting yourself and respecting your fellow professionals. Then there is the matter of how to keep on top of an industry where technologies and platforms are changing so fast. What might be the effect of AI and CGI on acting – or even on the need for actors? We hope that these exercises and the accompanying information will help you get ready for 'Action!'

To the tutor

As with any acting class, we would recommend that sessions start with relaxation, focusing and concentration exercises. Enthusiasm is a great dynamic to be working with, but students will get the most out of the exercises and games – and themselves – if they are calmly prepared for the tasks ahead. They can't all be in front of the camera all the time, and they need to have patience and enjoyment in the work of others as well as the buzz of flexing their own artistic muscles.

You will quickly become aware that many of the exercises have multiple applications and at times our allocation to certain skills may seem arbitrary – and in a way it is. We encourage you to adopt a holistic application of the exercises and to make connections across the different skills we have itemized.

We also recommend that tutors and workshop leaders take care to adjust the rules of engagement according to the age and maturity of the students. If physical touch or intimacy is to be allowed, it will be best to establish ground rules for this first, even though this runs the risk of setting up barriers or encouraging actors to prejudge the actions within a scene. Are any in the group in a relationship with each other? If so, can they accept what might happen in an improvisation or performance of a piece of text? Is it just a matter of 'what happens on set stays on set'? Any actor would find it difficult to watch whilst their loved one plays out a romantic scene with someone else. Similarly, it is distracting and inhibiting to try and play such scenes with your boyfriend/girlfriend/wife/husband in the room. Professional actors have to cope with such pressures all the time and the industry is littered with broken relationships as a result. Even though aspiring actors must ready themselves for such challenges whilst training, you will have to make a judgement call here based upon your knowledge of those under your guidance.

Equity UK issue a card which they recommend is read aloud at the beginning of every new project:

> Every single one of us working on this project is entitled to work in a safe space: a space free of fear, a space free of bullying and harassment of any kind. We will work together honouring our differences and celebrating the gifts we each bring to the table. We will treat one another with politeness and respect at al times and, if we are subjected to or witness bullying and harassment, we will speak out knowing that our voices will be heard and we will be taken seriously.
>
> Together we can create a Safe Space[3]

You may wish to use a similar pledge as you undertake the ideas in this book. For all our chapters we offer a tongue-in-cheek motto to summarize the work. This introductory chapter should be no different, but this motto is offered without irony.

Filmmakers' Motto:
Respect the work of others and celebrate difference.

[3]Issued 2018. Reproduced with the permission of Equity UK.

1 DON'T ACT, *BE!*

Working in theatre is like doing surgery with a scalpel. Working in film is like surgery with a laser.

MICHAEL CAINE[1]

To the actor

> The sooner the stage people who have come into pictures get out, the better for the pictures. (Marshall Neilan, actor/director/screenwriter (1891–1958), quoted in Brownlow 1973: 400)

Rather cruel, but it refers to the process that existed *before* sound recording was invented. During the silent cinema era, *c.*1891–1927, actors did actually speak on screen. It's just that without mics you can't hear them. Vocalizing helped them find the action. (In the same way, radio actors will often physicalize their studio performance in order to find the tone and colour of the text.) Emotions were presented physically, usually through a flurry of, at times, desperate pantomime:

> In 1908 the film producers and their audience derived the frame of reference primarily from their knowledge of theatrical conventions that were associated with the melodrama. (Pearson 1992: 7)

---

[1]'Michael Caine Teaches Acting in Film', YouTube.com, a 1987 BBC production, uploaded by FilmKunst, 5 November 2013. Available at: https://www.youtube.com/watch?v=bZPLVDwEr7Y [accessed 17 September 2018].

The beginning of film acting

When film acting first came into the picture (!) at the end of the nineteenth century, there were no dedicated drama schools in existence to help train actors for silent screen performance. Instead, seasoned professional stage performers were employed by the film studios and plonked in front of the newly invented motion picture camera. Some results appear disastrous, as the acting techniques seem to the modern eye manic and uncontrolled.

To help elicit passionate performances, directors resorted to various methods including the employment of professional musicians to create 'mood music'. This musical accompaniment was blasted out whilst the actors were in full-flight performance mode, for the days of post-production sound were still far away.

There were some advantages for the director, of course: they could direct loudly in conjunction with a wild mimicking of the gestures and emotions they were seeking from their actors. A recreation of this can be seen in Scorsese's *Hugo*. Such a process would not be tolerated today as it would completely ruin the actors' carefully built emotional interactions. Imagine Baz Luhrmann directing *Romeo + Juliet* (1996), screaming 'now kiss her!' whilst Leo DiCaprio holds Claire Danes in a sensitive passionate embrace. Probably not conducive to the carefully paced atmosphere of the scene.

To help narrate the story, silent film often used a title card: a printed piece of dialogue momentarily interspersed throughout the film to help the audience make sense of the visual images. To see a send-up of this style, a useful source is the classic 1952 *Singin' in the Rain* (Stanley Donen and Gene Kelly). One of its plotlines includes the transition from the silent to the newly arrived technique of the 'talkies' (ask your great-grandparents). But we should note that not all silent films are unbelievable or unwatchable due to an overcooked performance style – quite the opposite, and it is fascinating to watch the birth of naturalistic acting grow out of these early attempts at visual storytelling.

As an example of excessive acting style, we urge you to view a copy of the highly successful (in its day) *The Thief of Bagdad* (Raoul Walsh, 1924). Those who fancy a somewhat richer cinematic feast might like to sample Eisenstein's *Ivan the Terrible* (1944), an incredible piece of cinema, though out of sympathy with today's screen acting style. The horror-film monsters of the silent era that generated nightmares for a previous generation seem laughable to us today.

Now consider *The Crowd* (King Vidor, 1928), a landmark film that moves characterization (and screen performance technique) towards a more realistic representation. Over a twenty-year period, beginning in 1897, several areas of performance exploration and filmmaking converged to move the art of stage *and* screen acting towards a more *real* representation of emotions and storytelling. For actors, this began with the introduction of character construction acting techniques linked to the growth of understanding of psychology. These constructs were initially designed for the stage actor and were set out as a series of physical and internal exercises that strove to facilitate a more realistic and natural performance. This is the age of Ibsen and the realists. More natural styles of performance were facilitated by the arrival of electric light in the theatres that precluded the need for flamboyant gestures to penetrate the gaslight gloom. The artistic quest for this new realism would eventually transfer its passion for the clearest, deepest representation of human behaviour to the cinema.

The coming of 'The Method'

Just a quick dip into the codification of this new naturalism now – in case your stage-acting studies have managed to bypass it or you were thinking about something else at the time. In 1897 two Russian theatre practitioners came together over an eighteen-hour lunch meeting. They were Constantin Stanislavski (1863–1938) and Vladimir Nemirovich-Danchenko (1858–1943). The meeting is of historic significance to performance as both men had a desire to move theatre acting away from the melodramatic style of the period into a more psychologically and naturalistic-driven presentation. The outcome of this conversation was the birth of 'The Stanislavski System': a series of techniques designed to help construct believable emotions and actions. (We don't know who paid for the lunch.)

The System continued to adapt and grow and its influence led directly to the foundation in 1947 of New York's Actors Studio by Cheryl Crawford, Elia Kazan and Roger Lewis. They created a workshop where actors could discuss and experiment with acting techniques and performance. The American approach to the work of Stanislavski became known as 'The Method' and Lee Strasberg (1901–82) became its main figurehead and practitioner. Under his artistic direction, The Method developed into a renowned, fully immersive and intense framework for character creation. It was adopted by young theatre and screen actors such as Julie Harris, Marilyn Monroe, John Garfield, James Dean, Montgomery Clift and Marlon Brando. The Method developed their characterizations to become what we today know as 'natural acting'. From Stanislavski to Strasberg, plus encouragement by other directors such as Stella Adler and Elia Kazan, screen and stage actors began to understand and shape performance towards the required subtleties of the new medium. Actors, directors, scriptwriters, set designers and cinematographers were all beginning to engage with naturalistic visual storytelling.

The coming of sound

Since the invention of cinema, there had been experimentation with recording and lip-syncing to match the moving image, all with varying degrees of success and failure. In 1926, *Don Juan* (Alan Crosland) and *The Better 'Ole* (Charles Reisner) were released. Both had music and sound effects but no talking. Then came *The Jazz Singer* (Alan Crosland, 1927), the first full-length talking movie (though sound was present for only a quarter of the running time, with musical numbers – and silence – taking up the rest of the time). Films could now talk, and nothing would ever shut them up.

With their arrival, the microphone and recording equipment removed forever the possibility for film directors to direct a performance whilst the camera rolled. Sound capture became an integral and unavoidable working companion to film acting. Actors were suddenly challenged to produce vocal clarity and to act with neither the assistance of mood music, nor shouted instructions, nor audience feedback in the form of laughter or applause. It must have felt extremely lonely after a life on the boards.

Almost overnight, vocal coaching became a sub-industry, especially as the lure of stardom grew and the 'star system' became a tangible goal for fame-hungry performers. Countless would-be actors prepared themselves specifically for the 'talkies' to be their artistic home base and a few were talented (and lucky) enough to gain entry to this world of movie magic. Unfortunately, quite a few didn't make it and became, as is still the case, some of the most vocally trained waiters and waitresses in Hollywood.

From stage to screen

> Here is something no real celebrity will ever tell you: film acting is not very fun. Doing the same thing over and over again until, in the director's eyes, you 'get it right' does not allow for very much creative freedom … In terms of sheer adrenaline, film has absolutely nothing on theater. (Mara Wilson)[2]

Overall, the period from stage histrionics to naturalistic cinematic acting is not that long in the grand scheme of things, but it is an important journey to consider because the history of performance is one that you, training for this profession, can draw upon. You will be part of the next generation of innovations. Elements of screen acting require a different working approach from stage acting: a different understanding and modulation of voice and a different understanding and control of the body. Even the smallest gestures need highlighting on the stage lest the audience miss them: on film they are reduced to a minimum as the cine-camera will capture something as little as a throbbing vein. The audience has no choice but to follow the presented imagery. The theatre director has no such control over what the audience looks at. You may be giving a thunderous speech, but we may find that our gaze falls upon the actors receiving it. Moreover, the theatregoer will probably be able to do both: take in your speech whilst simultaneously absorbing the whole gamut of the stage action.

Alongside the microphone, the use of the close-up eliminates the need for many unnecessary physical movements and allows you, the actor, to concentrate instead on the inner life of the character as revealed by facial expressions. The use of the close-up rendered redundant many of the superfluous and 'actor-y' physical movements, facilitating instead a concentration on the interior life of the character, which the audience reads as they would read anyone's facial expressions in their own lives.

To experience the effectiveness of the close-up, consider Al Pacino (playing Michael Corleone) when he makes the discovery in a Havana nightclub of (spoiler alert) his brother's betrayal (sorry, too late!) in *The Godfather: Part 2* (Francis Ford Coppola, 1974). Pacino's stillness clearly

---

[2]Quoted on BrainyQuote.com. Available at: https://www.brainyquote.com/quotes/keywords/film_acting.html [accessed 1 December 2018].

conveys the inner turmoil of his character with minimum movement whilst optimizing dramatically the geography of his face, especially the eyes.

It may be of value to reflect on the characteristics listed below that help define the different working paradigms of stage and film. It is by no means complete and doubtless you will find entries for yourself as you discover the commonalities between the different media and, perhaps more importantly, the differences.

STAGE ACTING	FILM ACTING
Actors love acting on stage *and film*	Actors love acting on film *and stage*
Actors perform for a live audience	Actors perform for a camera
Actors perform in real time	Actors perform over a period of time
Actors' voices require projection	Actors' voices require natural levels
Actors 'find the light' on the stage	Actors 'hit the mark' on a film set
Actors' mistakes in full view but fleeting	Actors' mistakes hidden by editing
Actors have adequate rehearsal time	Actors have limited rehearsal time
Actors seek truth	Actors seek truth
Actors portray characters	Actors portray characters
Actors listen	Actors listen
Actors have control in performance	Actors lose control to director/ editor

Discuss these different characteristics (and any others you may discover) with the rest of the group. The more we discuss performances we have witnessed or taken part in, then the more we can understand each other and the art form we have chosen to study. Extend this to discuss screen performances you admire and why you admire them. By doing this you will naturally begin to break down the acting techniques (delivery and timing) of the professional actors who influence you the most. Suggest films to your colleagues and digest them together in shared study group and pizza sessions. What's your favourite scene (Why?) What's your favourite topping? (Doesn't matter why.) Take it in turns over the weeks and get that conversation about screen acting going!

> Whereas you can – and many effective actors do – get away with faking, posturing, and indicating emotions on stage, it's difficult if not impossible to get away with anything false before the camera. That instrument penetrates the husk of an actor; it reveals what's truly happening – if anything, if nothing. A close-up demands absolute truth; it's a severe and awesome trial. Acting for the screen is a more honest trade. (Kazan 1988: 257)

Just *be!*

For the screen actor, far more so than for the stage actor, it is necessary to hide the fact that you are acting. Many a director will have offered the (not always helpful) advice to 'Stop acting!' or 'I can see you acting!' or 'Just *be!*' What do they mean by this? Probably that they can see the mechanics of what you are doing. They see you *showing* us fear or anger or guilt or passion. The alternative is to marshal your thoughts, as the character, and to work from the inside by knowing your character as deeply as possible. (See the following chapter on backstory: Backchat.) We need to inhabit that character through processes we will discuss in the different chapters in this book. But the foundation of this preparation is Stanislavski's demand that we know our character, for then we will be better able to know how our character will behave. The key here is to consider how we *might* behave in a similar situation.

Stanislavski calls this the 'magic if'. This requires actors, once they have read and understood and interpreted the script, to ask themselves, 'What would I do if I were in my character's situation?' Your own physical movements, reactions and connections with the everyday may be a starting point for building your character's internal and external life. Or, through observation, you may inhabit the physical and vocal particularities of others, selecting those that most closely fit the description provided within the screenplay (which may include the character's job, emotional state, goals, successes, failures, loves and hates).

The 'Magic If' is a basic tool for naturalistic acting, whether for stage or screen. It consists of asking yourself the question 'if' I was this person/in this situation/at this time/wanting to achieve this objective – what would I do? Engaging with these questions opens up the creative possibilities for you as an actor in exploring and making real the character.

Take a moment here to consider and examine your own physical life in relation to objects, people and textures by analysing everyday gestures you use, such as:

- the extending of a hand for a handshake
- a nod of the head in agreement
- a shake of the head in disagreement
- a wave goodbye
- a hug hello.

Think about the gestures as you make them. For example, how do you turn the page of this book? How do you mark the page you have just finished so you know where to pick up next time? Do you bend the corners back? Do you use a bookmark? Are you reading and making notes at the same time? (Well, we had to ask!) Have you already given up and not even got this far? In which case, this question is pointless.

Physical life involves considering how the character moves, their physical gestures, their gait, their posture. This will be related to their backstory, their class, their employment, their age and the situation in which we see the character interact with others.

Apart from meditation or sleeping, which normally require us to remain still, our physical lives are driven by movements or gestures of some sort. It's the same for your character. Remember, each gesture is unique to you. Each one identifies you to your friends, family, fellow students, in fact everybody you know. Your gestures are real when you make them. And your character's gestures are real when you make them *for them.* That is what we strive for as actors: natural *actions* and *reactions* in response to dramatic situations whilst 'being' someone else. But every character you play incorporates and utilizes an aspect of yourself, and from that you cannot escape. Jeanne Moreau said, in an interview for *The New York Times*:

> Acting deals with very delicate emotions. It is not putting up a mask. Each time an actor acts he does not hide; he exposes himself.[3]

The 'Magic If' opens up more than this, for these movements and gestures stream from the panoply of emotions the character will experience, just as you do in your own life. You have to find and develop these aspects for the character in their 'real' life – the world created in the film or TV production (or the play). Did you ever tell a lie? How did it feel? Can you remember anything in particular, especially your physicality or facial control at the time? What if your character tells lies? Perhaps your character begins to talk faster in stressful situations and because of the lie? Or are they able to remain completely in control of the situation? Would their voices change somewhat? Maybe the pitch or breathing alters. Would they start to make speech errors, cough more, invent an itch the scratching of which excuses a partial obscuring of the face. Do they have a 'tell' when lying?

Or would nothing change at all? Would they stay perfectly calm whilst giving birth to the lie? Crucially, on film, do you as an actor 'show' us you are lying or try to conceal the lie in the manner of the character? The control lies (sorry!) in your head, the actor's head. As explained below, it is not that you are doing 'less' as a screen actor but that you have less need to demonstrate. Just be (the character). But it gets even more complicated. On stage there is a a plot device called 'dramatic irony' where the audience knows something that the character does not. Similarly, it may be that the director of the soap opera episode, of the police series or the hospital drama wants the viewer, but not the other characters, to know that the character is concealing something. Yes, complicated. Burt Reynolds tells a story about when, as a young TV actor, he found himself on the shooting set of an MGM movie, *Inherit the Wind* (Stanley Kramer,

---

[3]Interview with Jeanne Moreau, *New York Times*, 30 June 1976.

1961). The star of the film was the famous screen and stage actor Spencer Tracy, renowned for his natural approach to character, situation and environment. Reynolds reminisces about Tracy's advice to him regarding screen performing:

> Don't let anybody catch you at it. Don't act, just behave. (Loew 2010: 479)

In *The Silence of the Lambs* (Jonathan Demme, 1991), Anthony Hopkins' playing of Hannibal Lecter was based on choices he made. The *acted* calmness makes Hannibal all the more terrifying. Would it have been just as terrifying if Hopkins had played Hannibal in a manic, Hammer Horror fashion? The interpretation of the character works because the actor chose to play against stereotype. During his character construction period (pre-shoot), he would have considered carefully Lecter's gestures, which are clearly designed to flatter, deceive and seduce all the people within his character's world so that he can exert control over them. Hopkins uses this process to create very real and considered movements alongside the inner life of this most dangerous of cinematic creations.

Practising just being

Here's a couple of exercises you can try at home before working with your tutor and the group. They may help give you a little confidence and self-awareness before facing the camera.

> We are surprisingly unfamiliar with our bodies and many actors are inhibited about using them. Yet the body is the actor's primary instrument. To be brave and open requires a sentient and responsive body free from the limitations imposed by self-consciousness or fear. (Callery 2001: 22)

For the first one you will need a full-length mirror. Stand in front of the mirror and take in the image of your body. Be aware of how difficult and artificial this seems. Repeat, remembering to breath, and try to adopt a natural, relaxed position, not a pose for a selfie. Is it possible to be neutral? Does this feel awkward? Is it possible to stand there without 'making a face'? When we look at ourselves or when a camera is pointed towards us, we tend to pose. Take a look at the natural, non-posed photographs taken by Vivian Maier or Garry Winogrand (amongst countless others) and compare them to freshers' night-out photos. Is the group still and poised in the photo? Composed? Relaxed? Or leaning forwards – towards the camera – with multiple arms and lips in motion and making 'V for victory' signs as all engage in perfect pouting? We suspect the latter. It feels unnatural to be natural.

So, for this moment, patiently face the mirror with your own image staring back at you. No acting required. That's you. Right there. Now, you are looking at your very own and unique actor's playground. This is what you will present to casting directors eventually but, more immediately, it is what you will use in student workshops. It is the canvas upon which you will create your art. It is your starting point.

At first, you will see what you think are faults. Delete the word 'faults' and replace it with the term 'unique qualities'. If you do, you'll begin to treat your actor's playground as a malleable tool. It is important to be relaxed with *yourself*. What you are looking at now is pretty much what *we* see. This is also what the camera sees but with the addition of the character's complexities outlined in the script. Okay, that's enough of admiring yourself. How does one start to play in this wonderful actor's playground?

Make yourself a hot beverage. Clearly and methodically follow the action from the initial thought – your desire for a hot drink. What happens next?

- A series of muscle movements motor you from the mirror to the kitchen.
- Your eyes pinpoint the location of the tools you need to fulfil the action – i.e. tap, kettle, cup, spoon, sugar etc. Cookies optional.
- Your brain categorizes these objects as inanimate and in turn stimulates the central control system that kick-starts the physical actions required to manipulate them, leading to the desired conclusion: a cup of coffee.

You have an idea which turns into an objective and then you carry out physical actions to achieve that objective. On a basic level, this process is exactly the same for any character you are creating or presenting in performance to which you will have to add the character's particular circumstances. Go back to your starting place and try it again. This time you are *desperate* for that coffee as you are hung-over and worse, the cookie jar is empty. Or try being *angry* because someone has eaten your cookies.

Think about the missing cookies. Feel your annoyance about this theft growing. Now make the tea/coffee. Each time, notice what is happening as you move around the kitchen. How are you filling the kettle? How are you holding the cup? How are you drinking from it? Does the anger impact on your physicality? Scripts provide the dramatic stimuli that in turn affect physicality: for actors, that is where mind and body meet character.

So, you have now made your drink. Take a moment to enjoy it. Once finished, put everything you have used back in their original positions and don't forget to wash out the cup, especially if you are sharing an apartment. Forget about the cookies, they're bad for you.

Your objective is what you (the character) wants to achieve. What you do or say will be aimed at achieving that objective. You might enter the kitchen with the simple objective of getting a snack and be faced by a character whose objective is to murder you. Your objective will then change to one of survival. The clashing of different objectives from different characters is the energy of the drama.

As mentioned above, actors new to screen acting are often advised to 'do less' than they would on stage – but less than what? For some, that piece of advice becomes an immediate invitation to freeze both face and body when finding themselves in front of a camera with tutor and fellow students staring at them, all the while hoping that the character's inner emotions and conflicts will spontaneously spill out as if conjured up by some invisible magician. They won't. The 'do less' refers to 'containment'.

"Don't let your eyebrows upstage you! Most professional screen actors keep their eyebrows pretty still – the inclination to move them too much is very distracting for a viewer! – Sarah Leigh, actor

On stage, in front of a live audience, we need to hit the back row with both dialogue and physicality. For screen actors, the camera *is* the back row. Instead of doing less, we *contain* both movement and vocal delivery; the intention, determination and the intensity to portray the character is just the same for either medium but, in the cinema, an audience sees every line and crevice of your face on a twenty-foot high, fifty-foot wide screen. (Even bigger on an IMAX!) Under such a forensic gaze, there's no hiding place and the audience will know if you were thinking about your lunch whilst playing – or listening to your fellow actor playing – a very dramatic scene. In other words, if *you* are not concentrating, then the character is not concentrating, and the camera will capture that lapse.

Film and TV

Many actors will have their first screen opportunities on TV rather than film, and so a word or two about the differences. Many of the examples we give in this book are from film as generally these are easier for you to source. Increasingly, it seems that the worlds of TV and film are merging, with enterprises such as Netflix creating their own feature-length films for a home-viewing market. But there are subtle differences between acting for film and TV of which you should be aware. Film acting can (should?) be even more delicate than acting for the smaller screen. Your image is bigger and your expressions and reactions magnified. You will find that smaller reactions and responses can be read in film. This does not mean you are working less hard but, as stated above, that the intensity is more concentrated. Additionally, if your character is featured throughout the narrative, you have the time and space to live through your emotional journey; there is less pressure to fully establish your character before the commercial break!

> *"I was on holiday in Spain. Two days in, I got a call from my agent. The BBC was doing a play called* Shakespeare or Bust *by Peter Terson and someone had dropped out and would I play the part? The only snag was that I had to be at the read-through in Birmingham the following day and I was on a beach in Spain. I got*

up at three o'clock in the morning, flew to Barcelona and then on to Heathrow, where I was met and driven to Euston to catch a train to Birmingham. Another cab took me to the studios, where I experienced my first television read-through. I was in awe of those older actors who smoked and joked through the session. They were so relaxed. Afterwards, I remembered that my car was still in the car park at Gatwick airport. I had to be back in Birmingham to rehearse on location the following day, so I caught a train to Gatwick, then drove all the way back through Birmingham to Stoke.

Early the next morning, I was on a canal underneath Spaghetti Junction. I was jet-lagged, sleep-deprived and excited. My first television! What I hadn't realized was that rehearsals would be followed almost immediately by filming. My part was the owner of a boat hire company, who had to explain, using technical language, how a canal boat worked. During the rehearsal Brian Glover whispered to me, 'You haven't learned your lines, have you?' I said, 'I didn't know I would have to do it today.' I was used to lots of rehearsal and hadn't appreciated just how different television would be. This was turning out to be a bit of a nightmare. But Brian took me aside and we went over and over the scene together. With his kindness and encouragement and by the skin of my teeth, I survived and even got a mention in The Stage! *– Alan David, actor*

With the welcome exception of the BBC in the UK and channels like Arte in France and Germany, commercials structure modern TV shows. The plot, the moments of tension and the 'cliffhangers' will be built round the need to sell you a chocolate bar or a new car. It is during the commercial breaks that an audience is tempted to channel hop, and it is the director's duty to keep us tuned in to his show. In a cinema, you have paid your money and are unlikely to walk out of Screen One and pay to see the film in Screen Two instead. There will be pressure on the actor to make these pre-commercial moments as tense as possible. This may involve pausing, or holding a look rather longer than plausible and perhaps giving a somewhat unnatural weight to the line that takes us into the break. These moments involve an exaggerated emphasis that the TV actor will find useful, but the film actor will disown.

Having said that, there is much debate about whether the genres of screen and TV acting are merging along with the technology that produces them. Discussing the screening of live theatre events, Mark Shenton, in *The Guardian*, notes:

> The cinema audience may effectively watch a show from the best seat in the house, since that is where the cameras will be positioned; but the choices of what to look at will be made for you as well. Instead of watching from a fixed position, you will also be afforded different perspectives and close-ups that edit the experience for you. The actors, too, will be magnified and, more dangerously, so will their mannerisms – a performance that may be pitched to reach the back of the theatre can look over-the-top on camera. They can be amplified in voice, as well.[4]

In defence of this new acting hybrid, research by the National Theatre and the Tate asserts that:

> [C]inema audiences are more 'emotionally engaged' than theatre audiences. The clarity of sound and the intimate shots close to the actors' faces can make the experience more powerful. The intensity of theatre is still there but the character's emotions are captured more clearly.[5]

Screen acting is clearly changing and you, the actor, will have to adapt to survive; your relationship with the needs of the production via the director and assistant director (AD) will be crucial.

There are already an overwhelming array of house styles and genre mixes to which the screen actor must be able to adapt. On our screens we have police dramas with comedy, hospital dramas with comedy, police dramas and fantasy, romcom and fantasy. Programme makers are

---

[4]Mark Shenton and Hermione Hoby, 'Can a Filmed Stage Show Be as Good as the Real Thing?', *The Guardian*, 6 March 2011. Available at: https://www.theguardian.com/theobserver/2011/mar/06/national-theatre-live-frankenstein [accessed 13 February 2019].
[5]Zoe Nobileau, 'Live Theatre Screenings: A Curse or a Cure?', *The Boar*, University of Warwick, 23 March 2018. Available at: https://theboar.org/2018/03/live-theatre-screenings/ [accessed 13 February 2019].

always looking for a new cocktail. Each of these will require the television actor to adapt their techniques and talent in order to offer the required levels of emotional truth or comic timing and to fit into the style of the programme. If auditioning for a long-running series, be aware of the style whilst remaining alert to any clue that the director and writers might be seeking something different from you. In exercises throughout this book, you will have the chance to play around with these ideas. Neolithic alien hospital psycho-drama with comic undertones anyone?

To the tutor

Many of the exercises in this and subsequent chapters require the learning of short scenes. Some of these (such as the ones in this chapter) can probably be learned 'on the spot', but for longer scripts it may be advisable to divide students into groups and hand out copies of the text to both consider and learn a day or week before the performances are to be shot on film. Unless you have specific cause, extensive rehearsal should be discouraged, though line-runs are helpful.

The exercises that follow in this chapter are designed to allow the student of screen acting to experiment with the transition from stage to screen. Stanislavski was a great proponent of actors using their imagination and this should be encouraged whilst working within the disciplines of developing technique.

EXERCISE 1:1 THE WATCH

The student should read the script several times before rehearsing it.

A. I said I want your watch.
B. And I said, you can't have it!
A. I'll take it!
B. Don't mistake me for a victim.

The actors should note their responses to the following questions (all based on Stanislavski's System and discussed in more detail in the following chapter).

- Who am I?
- Where am I?
- When is the story set?
- What is going on?

Be alert to the fact that the obvious might not be the most interesting interpretation. How to look out for alternatives within a script is dealt with in later chapters, but note that this could be a street mugging, a domestic situation, an encounter in a care home or a scene from a spy movie (add your own possibilities here!).

Playback and discuss:

- What did the actors' faces *say* during the interaction?
- At the end of the delivery, did you think A would back down from B?
- Would A realize he/she has made a mistake in picking on the wrong person or would A end up with the watch?
- Who has the power?
- Did the power shift?
- How would *you* play the scenario?

Once the group has watched and thought about their screen work, they will realize that camera acting demands a different physicality than stage acting and is part of the interpretation of screenplay.

EXERCISE 1:2 FROM STAGE TO SCREEN

This exercise allows the student to chart the difference in performance requirements between stage and screen.

Take a short section of a stage script already known to the players, or alternatively create a short piece. For example:

A. I wasn't there.
B. I don't believe you.
A. You have to believe me. I was … somewhere else.
B. Really?

Play it as previously rehearsed for the stage or create a stage version of it. Place the players at one end of the room and the audience at the other. Repeat the performance over and over, with the audience getting closer and closer. Invite the actors to adjust the level of performance in response to the proximity of the audience. There will be an intermediary stage that resembles playing in the round. Increase this proximity to the point where the audience are in touching distance of the actors. Keep the essence of the scene the same – don't change the subtext during this exercise.

- What did the audience feel about the 'truth' of the performance?
- At what points did it seem especially to work or not work?
- How did it feel for the actors?
- What adjustments were they aware of making?
- Were any adjustments instinctive?
- Discuss the notion of concentration. Was there a qualitative difference as the audience approached?
- Discuss the vocal and physical technique used and how it changed during the exercise.

The scene can then be repeated for the camera. How subtle can the playing be now the camera takes over?

Variation. Exercise 1:2 can be replayed using key props, the significance or impact of which may differ from stage props. That the camera chooses to focus tightly on them tells us that the moment is significant. It is a technique often used by directors to 'flag' that an item or event is of significance to the plot. What if one of the characters is stirring a coffee or holding a letter? What if the camera picks out the fact that one of the characters is playing with their wedding ring? What difference does the biting of a lip or the flaring of a nostril create, or a mere blink? These would not be visible on stage but may feed the content of the scene. However, watch out for the trap of allowing such actions to be part of a demonstration of feelings rather than an outward reflection of inner turmoil.

EXERCISE 1:3 YOU DO KNOW HOW I'M FEELING

The vexed issue of the advice about 'doing less', 'don't act', 'stop showing me' and so on is a complex one for the training screen actor to gauge and modulate. As we have discussed, the outer is the product of the inner. How often in our own lives have we said (or had said to us) 'what's up?' when something is going on inside that is being reflected unwittingly on the outside.

Set up the camera and instruct the actor to enter the space and do nothing. As in the mirror exercise that students were invited to try earlier in the chapter, the task is to just stand there and do nothing. Let each student try this. Then play these back and ask what we, as an audience, are seeing. Is it 'nothing'? We will read *something* into the posture and facial expressions that the actor may or may not recognize as having been present. Because an audience is alert to interpreting what they see, even impassive, neutral physicality will be read as something.

EXERCISE 1:4 GETTING EMOTIONAL

This exercise can then be developed into an 'emotions' game. Given that we cannot be neutral, actors need to know what is going through their minds or preoccupying them at every moment as it affects their outer image. Again, ask the actor to strive towards being 'neutral' and then ask her to allow a certain memory to pass through her mind. You can trigger these ideas with questions:

- think about what you did last night
- think of a time when you were embarrassed
- think about someone you fear
- think about someone you like
- think of something that makes you angry
- think about that bill

- think about something you'd like to buy
- think about some difficult task you have to undertake.

Figure 2 shows, on the left, actors trying to be 'neutral' (Exercise 1:3). Look at the photos closely. The more you look, the more you will find yourself reading something into their (lack of) expression. The photos on the right show them responding to stimuli in Exercise 1:4. Which stimulus might each be responding to? The task is not about 'showing' a feeling, but feeling a feeling and allowing that to infect the expression.

FIGURE 2 Exercises 1:3 and 1:4 Actors doing 'nothing'? Photo by Luigi Caramella.

Shoot this in close-up: the actor will find that the tighter the shot, the less they have to do; the more they have to think and 'live through'. These short shoots should be reviewed with the group and supportively discussed as to their strengths and weaknesses. We don't all react the same way and our physicalities are all different. Every character played is an aspect of the actor. The discussions should recognize this and not imply that there is only one way of, for example, showing 'guilt'. Pay particular attention to the eyes. It is good training for actors to realize how much we read into what they give and receive.

Screen performances to consider

One of our favourite screen moments is from a 1926 silent film, *Ménilmontant* (Dimitri Kirsanoff). Although the opening scenes of this film contain levels of the stylized heightened performance now out of fashion, towards the end there is a scene of startling subtlety between a starving young girl and a down-at-heel older man. They are sharing food and the performance of the young girl (uncredited) is supremely internalized.[6]

Another silent classic worth your attention is the early vampire movie *Nosferatu* (F. W. Murnau, 1922). Other silent classics to research and review would include *Ivan the Terrible* and *The Cabinet of Doctor Caligari* (Robert Wiene, 1922). Or if you really want to go back to the beginnings, have a look at Georges Méliès' 1902 fantasy *A Trip to the Moon*.[7]

Here is a list of some of our favourite films where the artistry is underpinned by solid characterization that lingers in the memory. Film acting methodologies are varied but the individual approaches converge to create memorable, cinematic arcs of storytelling. The list is subjective, but you will find it both diverse and informative.

---

[6] The scene in question can be found at: https://www.youtube.com/watch?v=5guIdpsclnI. The full film (38 minutes) can be found at: https://www.youtube.com/watch?v=DHQH9DoO0gk [accessed 18 September 2018].

[7] Available at: https://www.bing.com/videos/search?q=Lumiere+brothers+a+trip+to+the+moon+&&view=detail&mid=EC235E8EE7B7BC406723EC235E8EE7B7BC406723&&FORM=VRDGAR [accessed 18 September 2018].

- Bruno Ganz in *Downfall* (Oliver Hirschbiegel, 2004)
- Jeon Do-yeon in *Secret Sunshine* (Chang-dong Lee, 2007)
- Joaquin Phoenix in *The Master* (Paul Thomas Anderson, 2012)
- J. K. Simmons in *Whiplash* (Damien Chazelle, 2014)
- Viola Davis in *Fences* (Denzel Washington, 2016)
- Isabelle Hubbert in *Elle* (Paul Verhoeven, 2016)

What have *you* seen that excites you enough to want to enter this world of make-believe? What films stick out for you and why?

> In the theatre you can change things ever so slightly; it's an organic thing. Whereas in film you only have that chance on the day, and you have no control over it at all. (Judi Dench)[8]

Screen Actors' Motto #1:
Use my feet, but walk in the character's shoes.

---

[8]Interview with Chris McKittrick, *Daily Actor*, 15 October 2012. Available at: https://www.dailyactor.com/broadway-theater/judi-dench-theater-film [accessed 4 October 2018].

2 BACKCHAT: CREATING A BACKSTORY

Every scene you will ever act begins in the middle, and it is up to you, the actor, to provide what comes before.

SHURTLEFF 2009: 48

To the actor

Backstory. You may have a great deal of information about your character from the script or even other relevant research. It will help you define your objectives and motivations if you are aware of these, which you can then develop into a fuller 'backstory'. Depending on the script, you may have a great deal of leeway to create this backstory, but you must also make sure it fits with the requirements of the film. Don't be too indulgent.

That, in brief, is 'backstory'. It is a concept that will come up frequently in this book so we are going to consider what it might mean and how you can set about piecing one together. Even the smallest role will benefit from you having an understanding of the character's past, their world view, their financial and emotional situation. We are accustomed these days to talk about people having 'baggage': the events that have affected – even scarred – them in the past. Creating a backstory is about finding the character's baggage and carrying it with you into the role. In this process you should find an empathy with the character – an understanding of what makes them tick. What do you like in the character, what similarities are there between you and them? Are there any aspects of your own personality that even marginally relate to them? Can you find some point of empathy with them, even if they're a mass murderer?

Needless to say, if you are taking up a major role, the detail of the backstory will have to be broad and deep. You, the actor, will carry this baggage, though your character may be ignorant of it. Once identified and absorbed, it is there and feeds your imagination, your actions and reactions as you play the scenes. Actors are often encouraged to utilize their own memories to help this process, usually referred to as using 'emotion memory'.

Emotion memory involves recalling from your own life an incident when you felt the same range of emotions. This will help you identify with the character and more accurately reproduce the required actions and reactions using emotional recall.

A health warning. Using deeply personal and traumatic memories can be dangerous to your mental health! You, the actor, must remain in control lest you slip into your character's reality completely. Do not allow yourself to become overwhelmed by personal memories. Stanislavski stresses that art is a product of the *imagination* and we would recommend that you trigger relevant emotions through the use of your creative imagination inspired by such situations:

> The aim of the actor should be to use his technique to turn the play into a theatrical reality. In the process imagination plays by far the greatest part. (Stanislavski 1949: 31)

The first level of establishing this backstory is to focus on the facts as presented by the screenplay. From the words on the page:

- What do you know about the character from what they say?
- What do you know about the character from what they do?
- What do you know about the character from what other characters say about you? (And are they right?)
- What you *think* you know – what does your instinct tell you?
- What is not there and you really need to find out?

Having established all this, you can go on to:

- Define your baggage.

The building blocks of backstory

Let's look at this in a little more depth. Starting with the details in the screenplay and then moving beyond them with the help of your imagination and research, you are trying to create a coherent and believable performance. The purpose of this imaginative research is to answer the following questions:

- Who am I?
  Who is the character you are playing? What do they wear? What is their history? What has made them who they are? Use the script, your instincts and imagination, but keep it real. We are encouraging you to be inventive but not completely off the wall. Don't invent a grandparent locked in the attic unless there is a really good reason.

- Where am I?
  Does your character like where she is? Physical surroundings affect character. Pay attention to the script: don't play living on Jupiter if it's set in Jakarta.

- When is the story set?
  What season? What year? If the information is not in the stage text or the workshop film script, find out. (And be prepared: that summer beach scene may be shot in mid-winter.)

- What is my character's motivation?
  What exactly is the engine driving your actions? Your motivation is what drives you and you pursue it by means of a series of objectives.

- Why do I want it and is it worth the trouble?
  Is it to escape something? Someone? The past? The present? The future? Yourself? What is it that pushes the character onwards? How significant is it? Could you let it go? It must have importance for the character to conduct themselves as they do.

- How will I get it and how will it affect me if I don't get it?
  How will the character get what is wanted? Guile? Pretence? Violence? Love? A clear goal will help to keep you on the right track. You say what you say and do what you do as a means of achieving your goal.

- What do I need to overcome in order to triumph?
  What or who has the power to stop you achieving your objective? What do you have to do to resolve this?

You don't have to create a world that encompasses every second since birth but establish anchor points. Backstories can be minimal or extensive. The decision of how far you delve is yours. But even the most minuscule details will help your character have a life *before* the scene you are currently engaged with. As a result you will go onto the set knowing exactly what experiences from the past have informed this moment. Although buried deeply, they are the engine that drives your character and motivates them. When interruptions to the shoot occur, this internal country of the backstory will be an attractive place to visit to regain your focus. Decisions you make about education, health and emotional security will affect the vocal and physical life of the character. It's a complicated recipe that you have to cook to perfection.

> As far as preparation goes, it's important to understand the who, what, where, why of the character before you meet him. That helps the character employ those tactics for whatever action they're trying to perform, which can necessitate a limit of choice as well as a discovery of new things to be learned as an actor to portray the character with. (Benedict Cumberbatch)[1]

Perhaps you have been asked to play a character who was born in Good Grief, Idaho. Yes, this is a real place. Like us, you have probably never heard of Good Grief, Idaho, unless of course you come from there, in which case you will find the following exercise very easy to do. First, find Good Grief on an online map. Then:

---

[1]'Benedict Cumberbatch Webchat: Your Questions Answered on Kung Fu, a Wayward Cloak and Going Shirtless', *The Guardian*, 24 October 2016. Available at: https://www.theguardian.com/film/live/2016/oct/24/benedict-cumberbatch-answers-your-questions-live [accessed 1 December 2018].

- Locate a particular street.
- Locate a school, a cinema, a restaurant. All the things you yourself would have seen or experienced when you were growing up. Imagine the same for your character.

This will be the place you go to in your imagination to create and maintain your character, crafting a story arc that lays down markers to guide you through situations as required.

> I write a bio of the character. I try to fill it up as much as possible. What are her memories? Does she have brothers and sisters? What secrets does she have? What's her favorite color? I do all of that work first. (Viola Davis)[2]

Let's take an example. You are up for a leading part in a remake of Harper Lee's *To Kill a Mockingbird*. It could be Atticus Finch, or Scout or Tom Robinson. The first thing you would do, of course, is read the screenplay (if available to you) and the book (if you haven't already. If you have, read it again – it's not *that* long). You might also be tempted to watch Gregory Peck, Mary Badham and Brock Peters in the 1963 version (Robert Mulligan) – but it might be better to avoid this influence if you are going to bring your own interpretation to the part.

Reading the source material is just the beginning. You will need to know about and understand the political, social, economic and racial context of the events. For the sake of example, we'll consider Atticus. From the written material, you will know what he does (defends Tom Robinson against a false charge of rape) and be aware of the moral values he lives by and tries to instil in Scout, his daughter. You will discover, for example, that Scout's mother died when she was two years old and that she was fifteen years younger than her husband, which made the death unexpected. What might have been the effect on Atticus of this loss? How might the world view of Scout and her relationship with her father been affected by this? A whole Pandora's box of questions follows about his own childhood, schooling, wealth, religion and moral development. How

[2]'Viola Davis on Acting', interview, Guru.Bafta.org, 1 February 2017. Available at: https://www.youtube.com/watch?v=a-f4DDnGSBc [accessed 1 October 2018].

does he see himself and how does he wish others to see him? What is happening in Atticus's world which may affect him? How did he cope as a single father? Figure 3 illustrates some of the possible components of such a backstory, the source of which would be the screenplay, the original book, sociological and political research – and your own instincts and imagination.

Ensure that you are involved in a deeper exploration of the screenplay and not contradicting it. The book contains many speeches and insights that the screenplay will try to convey in other ways – through body language, reactions, what is left unsaid, as well as through the art

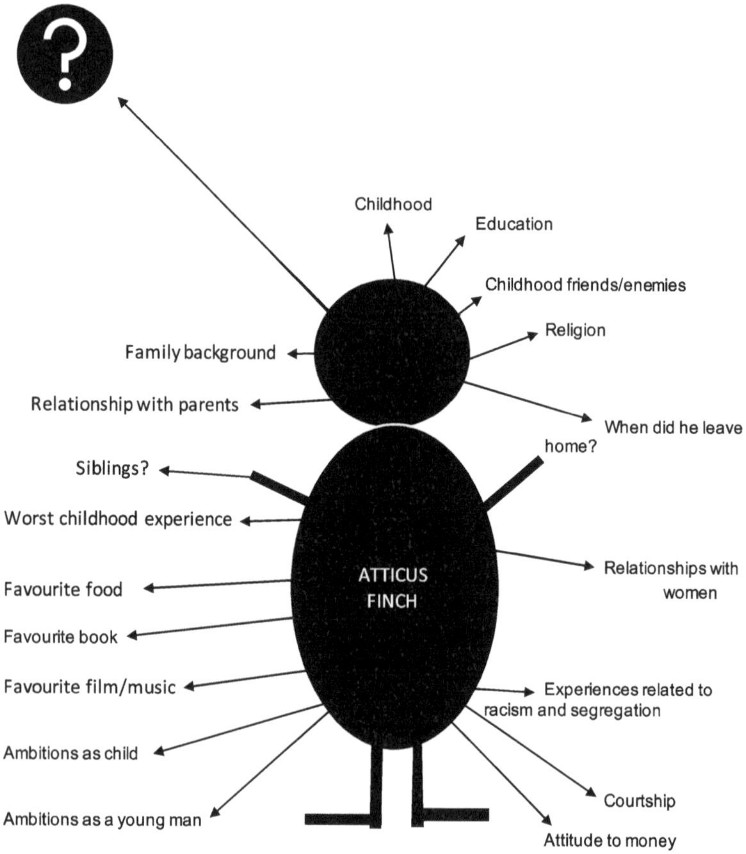

FIGURE 3 Examples of components for a backstory. Courtesy of Simon Hyland.

direction and musical score. The words unspoken are not only filled by your backstory, they are created by it.

In our example you need to decide what motivates Atticus (or Scout or Tom) to do what they do and say what they say. What do they 'want' to happen in each scene – what are their objectives? How does Atticus pursue his objectives inside and outside the courtroom? What are his previous circumstances?

Given or Previous Circumstances. This is from Stanislavski again and relates to creating your backstory. The given circumstances are what you know, from the script (what you say, what you do, what other characters say about you). They underpin your portrayal of the character.

It may even be that in this new version of *To Kill a Mockingbird* the screenwriter and director wish to reflect the new information about Harper Lee's creation revealed in *Go Set a Watchman*, in which Atticus is portrayed as an apologist for racist ideology and a supporter of educational segregation. Voting is a right to be earned – 'a precious privilege' (2015: 244). 'Do you want them in our world?' he asks. Could you present a *Mockingbird* version of Atticus that takes account of this flirtation with the Ku Klux Klan?

Given circumstances

Such given circumstances may have a direct, immediate and overwhelming impact on your performance.

"I was working on a drama playing the part of someone with motor neurone disease. Unusually in TV, as part of my contract I was able to carry out some research and meet two women at different stages of the disease. This became an invaluable experience for me: talking about their experience and getting an

insight into the effects on the body. I then had a day with the actor playing my son/carer in the drama. The director was very helpful in working through some of the blocking for the scenes and this is where my actor training really empowered me. We worked with Alexander Technique – I had an idea that if my son/carer and I could work physically on holding me and carrying me, this would help. The director watched as we slowly became physically more intimate with each other, cutting through the initial reservations that we may have had on set. And also because it was Alexander Technique, it kept us both safe from harm or injury. For actors without an understanding and training in physical awareness, the whole process may have taken much longer and been quite embarrassing as an older women working with a young actor who was physically going to carry me, wash my hair tenderly and get me out of bed etc. as the script demanded. – Ava Hunt, actor

In Chapter 8 we deal with the problems of shooting out of sequence and maintaining your superobjective. We make special reference to Robert Donat's Emotion Chart (Figure 14) and this work on backstory is an essential precursor to charting truthfully your journey through the story of the screen production.

In the genre of biographical film, the characters (or at least the key ones) come complete with their backstories. The actor, when dealing with real stories, usually has a wealth of biographies to peruse as research. There is no point in making up a fictional backstory for Gandhi or Erin Brockovich when the real one already exists – ready to be interpreted by you. But you may still have to work out the motivations!

To the tutor

It will be obvious that the application of backstory could be applied to the majority of the exercises in this book. Virtually every piece of dialogue or improvised situation allows for the actor to consider the 'baggage' the character is bringing to the studio floor. We include three exercises here expressly designed to help develop backstory, but we recommend that you urge your students to engage with this fundamental work and to keep a record of it to which they can add ideas and amend others.

EXERCISE 2:1

Present them with a character from a play and ask them to create a backstory on the lines of the Atticus example above. Hot-seat this character and then share the backstory with the group and discuss what might be the implications for a performance of that character.

Variation. Set the task of writing an obituary for the character, outlining the achievements and failures of his life.

EXERCISE 2:2 CLINT EASTWOOD'S CHAIR

We have named this exercise after a famous incident at a political rally in 2012 where Eastwood threw questions at an empty chair and answered them himself. He imagined aiming his questions at the then presidential candidate Barack Obama. We take that improvised real-life moment and extend it.

There is an empty chair. 'A' is desperate to get something off his/her mind. They want to say something important but the person they want to say it to is not present. How they relate the important information is A's inner dilemma, and he or she 'rehearses' the delivery by pretending the other person is sitting in the chair.

A. How dare you! I know what it means, what it really means!

The actor repeats this several times in front of the workshop participants in different ways, both vocally and physically. They then choose one recitation they feel is right and keep this choice to themselves. The tutor invites B to fill the empty chair and the camera is ready to roll. After 'Action!', A decides whether to pause before the line:

FIGURE 4 Exercise 2:2 Clint Eastwood's chair. Photo by Abby Timms.

A. How dare you! I know what it means, what it really means!

'Cut!' is called after thirty seconds, allowing time for B to respond through a facial reaction alone. The shot footage is screened and discussed.

- Why did you think A chose that way of delivery?
- Why did you think B responded in the way they did?
- Was the physicality of both characters conveyed before the line delivery?
- What was B's reading of A's face before the line was delivered? Were there indicators that signalled impending bad news?
- How would you play the scene?
- What do you presume the backstory of the characters to be?

The exercise is repeated with other students, using a different text if necessary.

EXERCISE 2:3 WHAT DO YOU MEAN?

This exercise requires learning a short monologue, so should be presented to the students in advance. The students are asked to find a short speech from a play, a film, newspaper or magazine article. The adventurous types can write something. The only proviso is that it should not be something the class has heard before – so no Gettysburg Address or Quint's emotive USS *Indianapolis* speech from *Jaws* (Steven Spielberg, 1975). The exercise is aimed at gaining *ownership* and developing appropriate backstory.

The cohort sit in a semicircle around two chairs facing inward to each other. Two students are 'volunteered' and they sit facing each other. One is the deliverer. One is a questioner. The questioner can only ask one question – 'What do you mean?' (though they can ask it multiple times) – and they must listen very carefully to what is said. The deliverer must answer as truthfully and convincingly as possible. We are going to cheat and use a famous speech as an example.

Hamlet: To be, or not to be, that is the question:
Whether 'tis nobler in the mind to suffer
The slings and arrows of outrageous fortune,
Or to take arms against a sea of troubles
And by opposing end them. To die – to sleep,
No more; and by ....
Questioner (interrupting): What do you mean?
Hamlet: Well, actually ...

Hamlet has to explain what he means based on the questioner's inquisitiveness. The exercise puts the deliverer on the spot as they search out a truthful answer – culled from imagination and *backstory*. The question can be asked multiple times at any point. At the end of the exercise the group gives feedback as to whether they believed the answers – or not. In other words, was there evidence of a coherent backstory underpinning the answers? The purpose of the exercise is not to catch the student out but to sharpen their *ownership* of the text.

Screen performances to consider

We won't insult potentially litigious actors by pointing out examples of weak backstories. Instead, have a look at the following four biopic recommendations and after viewing do a little research yourselves into the real characters' backgrounds. You will be following the work undertaken by the actors involved. What choices did they make and what motivations did they have to establish?

- *Lady Sings the Blues* (Sidney J. Furie, 1972) with Diana Ross as jazz entertainer Billie Holiday.
- *Raging Bull* (Martin Scorsese, 1980) with Robert De Niro as the boxer Jake La Motta.
- *Frances* (Graeme Clifford, 1982) with Jessica Lange as the actress Frances Farmer.
- *Face of an Angel* (Martha Coolidge, 1999) with Halle Berry as the singer Dorothy Dandridge.
- *La Vie en Rose* (Olivier Dahan, 2007) with Marion Cotillard as the singer Edith Piaf.

Screen Actors' Motto #2:
Keep your character's baggage with you but out of sight.

3 THE ACTOR AS PLUMBER

[Y]ou come, and you do your scenes in a few days, and you act with a couple of colleagues. All the rest of the actors you never see, and you don't even meet many of them. And you don't know what will happen with what you've done. Maybe it will be in the film, maybe it will not.

MAX VON SYDOW[1]

To the actor

Behave yourself

Where are you going? It's a question that your Stanislavski studies will have encouraged you to ask of any character you are playing. It is the 'Who am I? Where am I? Where am I going?' of the previous chapter. But 'Where are you going?' is a question screen directors don't like to ask; they are more likely to say, 'Go over there'. This will not be a random whim but rather a direction based on thoughtful preparation by the director to get you into a position that allows your character to have the required impact. This will not be the time for you to say, 'Eh … my character wouldn't move *there*.' Rather, it is the time to take the position requested and, no matter how odd or uncomfortable it feels, *to make it work.*

> All the time, all around you is a babble of these little instructions, from crew to crew from director to cameraman. When you come onto a sound stage it sounds like bedlam, but it can be sorted out easily – if you know how. (Astor 1997: 187)

---

[1]Quoted on BrainyQuote.com. Available at: https://www.brainyquote.com/authors/max_von_sydow [accessed 25 July 2018].

This is not to say that directors always treat actors like puppets. Input into the scene may have been asked for in a rehearsal – if there has been one! It is at *that* point that it may be appropriate to offer suggestions on character, but character only. Don't be tempted to tell the director that they have the camera placed in the wrong direction to capture your 'best side'. You are part of a team and your job is solely to present your performance.

> I think you should take your job seriously, but not yourself. That's the best combination. (Judi Dench)[2]

You are there to do a job and it is no more important than any of the other jobs being done around you. The golden rule is that the director has artistic control and the actor is subservient to that control. The director, cinematographer and ultimately the editor make the final choices – not the actor. For actors more accustomed to the free discussions of a devising process or theatre rehearsal, this can be a real shock to the system, especially your egosystem. How to do your job:

- Always arrive early for a shoot and make allowances for possible transport delays. When you are a star (but not before), they will send a limo, any colour you want. Until then, be reliable.
- If you are playing a small part and the main lead is, for example, Clint Eastwood (insert any star of your choice), don't be tempted to engage them in conversation as their minds are probably on a million other things.
- Be respectful and courteous.
- Don't be tempted to pick up a prop bow and arrow or gun and start playing around. Food that is part of the setting is not a buffet and may not even be edible.
- Keep all conversations off set unless initiated by the director or cameraperson. Quietly wait for instructions.
- Moving any form of equipment will probably get you thrown off a set. It's not your job.

[2]Quoted on BrainyQuote.com. Available at: https://www.brainyquote.com/quotes/judi_dench_299846 [accessed 25 July 2018].

- Always be clear as to your position in relation to the camera. If in doubt, gently get the attention of the AD and ask.
- You may check with the AD or cameraperson about the 'tightness' of the shot.
- Nobody has any interest in how famous you think you are going to be. Your job as the actor is to be there and to do a job.
- Even though you film your scene or scenes, and get paid for them, there is no guarantee whatsoever that you will make it to the final cut and a public screening. Don't be disheartened: this happens a lot and it will have nothing to do with your performance but with practical decisions made by the editor and the director.

If your scene does get cut, you're in good company:

- Harvey Keitel cut from *Apocalypse Now* (Francis Ford Coppola, 1979)
- Kevin Costner cut from *The Big Chill* (Lawrence Kasdan, 1983)
- Ashley Judd cut from *Natural Born Killers* (Oliver Stone, 1994)
- Uma Thurman cut from *Savages* (Oliver Stone, 2012)
- Jennifer Jason Leigh cut from *Eyes Wide Shut* (Stanley Kubrick, 1999)
- Mickey Rourke cut from *The Thin Red Line* (Terrence Malick, 1999)
- Robert Pattinson cut from *Water for Elephants* (Francis Lawrence, 2011)
- Toby Maguire cut from *Life of Pi* (Ang Lee, 2012)

Working with the screenplay

The screenplay is a working map guiding you towards a resolution not just of how the story ends but how the actor should approach the character as presented on the page by the writer. In other words, the actor takes fictional situations and presents a coherent performance by serving the script and exploring choices that are not necessarily true to life, but that are consistent with the story or the given circumstances through research and rehearsal. This is the backstory discussed in the previous chapter. Further, your contribution must fit into the jigsaw of pieces made up of your own work and that of the other actors.

The Celluloid Stew

> What are the most important things that you want to know about actors you're considering? [JS]
>
> All I care about is how well they act. (Director Sydney Pollack, quoted in Stevens 1997: 21)

Take an idea, throw in plot, genre, acting, money, lights, context, sound, history, publicity, weather, money, costume, location, money, food, transport, script changes, arguments, artistic differences, money, casting, miscasting, and even more money. This is the Celluloid Stew. And when an actor walks into an audition, the director will assume that because he has got this far in the casting process that they are completely aware of what is required. Otherwise, why would the agent send them? It is only when it goes wrong that the director and crew begin to pull out the hair from their collective toupees and start to question why they hired this person in the first place.

There are several reasons why it could go wrong, such as:

- The agent signed up the actor after seeing them give a magnificent performance on stage and assumed, because talent was visibly burning bright on the boards, that *all* aspects of acting would be similarly ready to shine.
- Nerves set in when confronted by the technology and the operators who seem to *live* on the set, and who are totally unimpressed by the fresh-faced novice. The actor realizes suddenly that she is a very small cog in this machine and confidence melts away under the heat of the lights and a stomach-knot of insecurities.

The bottom line is this: when we walk into a professional audition or onto a set, we must walk in as a professional ready to do a job. There is no other option. That is why we want you to consider the actor as 'plumber'.

> For me, our job as artists is to serve the story, serve the director, and serve the fellow actors. And if you do that, by osmosis you're serving yourself because you'll get the best out of yourself. (David Oyelowo)[3]

You hire a plumber to install the heating system. They arrive. They do the job. They leave. And we expect the heating to work. If it doesn't, you will never hire that plumber again. The same goes for an actor who fails to carry out his job with competency. Acting is a profession and if the professional trust is lost, the working relationship and the work will end – very quickly.

> *"On set – and before, in the make-up room and costume department – you are working with a whole range of extremely skilled people doing complicated jobs and you are just one small part of it. – Philip Bird, actor*

Actors need to *cultivate* the skills (we are not born with them) that are necessary for breaking down a script and putting it back together so that it will work effectively for a director, camera and audience. You must also sharpen all aspects of your own technique and similarly pull those back together in coherent performance.

During your training is the time to identify your weaknesses. Only then can you mitigate the inevitable rush of emotions when you step in front of a camera for the first time on an organized shoot.

- I'm not ready.
- I don't like this.
- I can't remember my lines.
- I don't like that camera in my face.
- I don't like my face.
- I want to be a dentist.

---

[3]'David Oyelowo Brings MLK to Life in "Selma"', interview with Mark Peikert, Backstage.com, 14 January 2015. Available at: https://www.backstage.com/interview/david-oyelowo-brings-mlk-life-selma/ [accessed 25 July 2018].

Valid reactions for the first time on a shoot, but they need to be overcome so that you become more in control of self and character. Use your time in the training environment to prepare for this.

> Why do I always freeze? Shit! I went through the war. I jumped out of bombers. I played kick-the-can with E-boats when all we had was a lousy forty-foot dragger with six machine guns and a top speed of six knots. Yet whenever I get a close-up in a nice warm studio, I curl up and die. (Hayden 1998: 365)

That is quite a statement coming from a seasoned six-foot-five actor who appeared in seventy-two feature and television films, especially when one recalls that Sterling Hayden was involved in one of the most infamous mixtures of mid- and close-up shots ever committed to celluloid: the assassination of Captain McClusky (played by Hayden) by Michael Corleone (Al Pacino) in Francis Ford Coppola's *The Godfather* (1972).

> *"Screen acting is more technical [than stage acting] and therefore something that can be learned and improved upon over time. It's always a good idea to confirm the type of shot the director wants so that you can adapt your movements and expressions. A mid-shot may give you a bit more freedom but a close-up may mean a more subtle smile. It's good to be aware of the framing but don't let this determine your performance – always go with your impulse as you would on stage. If it looks too much on camera, an experienced director will simply ask you to adjust for the next take. – Robin Kirwan, actor*

Ready for 'Action!'

Anyhow, you've got your first screen acting job. At the centre of the studio bedlam you sit, silently shaking, lips forming invisible words, trying to remember lesson six (or was it lesson seven?) that workshopped Stanislavski's inner monologue technique … or was that Stella Adler … or Strasberg? Then somebody, in all innocence, moves the monitor to a place where everyone can see the screen – including a young actor who now sees herself in glorious close-up. Glorious! Except for … the nose. (Substitute any physical feature at this point.) The young actor now becomes fully conscious of her proboscis. Stanislavski, Adler, Strasberg, a plastic surgeon even, cannot help now. It's too late. The carefully prepared inner life of the character becomes lost in the miserable mist of self-loathing, all because of a perceived facial flaw.

Inner Monologue. We do not say everything that passes through our minds (thankfully!), but what we actually say and do as a character will be the result of what is going on inside their head. You need to be aware of this inner monologue whilst at the same time hanging on to the controlling processes of you the actor.

Although it involved another part of the head entirely, we witnessed something similar on a student shoot. The crew had set up for a 360-degree shot around a young actor, who happened to glance at the monitor during a rehearsal, where he saw an unmistakable bald patch – in its infancy but definitely and proudly announcing itself on a 32-inch monitor to a concerned audience of – one … the actor. Nobody else cared. Until, that is, the shoot began again; this time a take. The actor delivered the lines but it became obvious to all that something had mysteriously clouded an otherwise excellent portrayal. 'Cut!' was called but no amount of gentle direction could pull this actor from his misery. We tried to reassure him that acting is for all shapes, sizes – an exclusive membership to an industry that celebrates differences. We advised the young actor to look at the films of Yul Brynner, Telly Savalas, Bruce Willis, Sean Connery … but to no avail. He was not for turning and, sadly, never again stood in front of a film camera.

> I don't really like watching my stuff. It makes me feel sick. You imagine you look a certain way in your head, and when it looks even the slightest bit different from what you imagine, you go, 'Rubbish!' (Robert Pattinson)[4]

---

[4]'Robert Pattinson – Biography', *Hello!* magazine. Available at: http://www.hellomagazine.com/profiles/robert-pattinson/ [accessed 25 July 2018].

Preparing for your first shoot

You've got the script and memorized the lines. Your confidence will be underpinned by your preparation.

- What does the character say? Why? Is there a subtext?
- You have read the whole script so that you know not only what *they* say but also what other characters say *about them*. Is this information reliable? Do other characters have motives behind their words?
- You glean all possible information about the character – who/what/where/when/why.
- You have considered a backstory (see Chapter 2) that accommodates all these facts.
- You have considered the physical life of the character that accommodates the backstory.

Subtext. We do not say all we mean and we often mean something other than the apparent import of the words we use. 'Is there any cheese in the fridge?' might actually mean 'Will you make me a sandwich?'. 'You are the most unusual person I've ever met' could mean 'You're weird' or 'You're intriguing'. It is related to inner monologue, and you will have to make decisions about the subtext of all you say.

The day of the shoot – a checklist

- You have got up in good time and arrived at the location.
- You took especial care with personal hygiene that morning and carry breath mints.
- You have turned off (not just put on 'silent') your mobile phone.

- You wait. Interminably. Probably 95 per cent of the time on set will be spent waiting. You've taken a book. Or you spend time meeting fellow actors – maybe for the first time.
- If you have rehearsal time with the director or AD, you are prepared to adjust your preconceptions of the character to what is required.
- Eventually, you will be required on set for angles, lighting and sound checks. *You wait.*
- The AD requires 'Quiet on set'. Even if you are not in this shot, this means absolute silence, no whispering, no turning the page of your book and no rustling in a bag for a chocolate bar. *You wait.*
- The AD checks that sound and camera are ready. 'Sound ready?' You concentrate totally. The sound operator answers, 'Sound ready'. 'Camera ready?' The camera operator replies, 'Ready!' *You wait.*
- The AD announces 'Roll sound'. The reply comes back: 'Rolling. Speed.' Then 'Roll camera'. The response comes back: 'Rolling. Speed.' *You wait.*
- The clapperboard operator announces the scene and take and 'marks it'.
- You and the other actors are ready. *You wait.*
- The director says 'Action!'
- You breathe, leave a beat, and begin. To jump in immediately on 'action' risks starting on the wrong emotional level and may create problems for the editor later.
- As you work on the (say) two-shot, you are noting at what point you look at the other actor, when you flick the cigarette or take a drink. It will be necessary to reproduce these actions in the subsequent angles yet to be shot.
- The scene doesn't end until the director says 'Cut!' Even if you make an error or drop a line (or a handkerchief), you must cope with the situation, live through the moment in character and recover. You must keep going unless the director shouts 'Cut!' Maybe the 'error' is a moment of truth or serendipity that the

director thinks she may want to keep. Or maybe other parts of the take have been good and the director is confident he can work round the 'error' in editing. The actor does not make this decision. The director decides. Above all, the take doesn't end when the last line of the scene has been spoken! Some of the most effective moments can arise in the silence between actors at the end of a scene. Keep acting. An experienced director will leave some space at the end of the scene to allow 'wriggle room' for the editor. Likewise, even after 'Cut!', it is good practice to leave a 'beat' before relaxing out of character.

- You then await instructions for the next take, shot or angle. You pay close attention to any instructions and maintain your concentration. And you wait.

> *"I once did an infomercial for a security firm playing a burglar trying to break into somebody's house. I just lurked outside holding a flashlight for maybe ten or twenty seconds. That was it. I waited on set each night for three consecutive nights before they finally got around to filming my part. It was great, though, because for twenty seconds of lurking they had to pay me for three full days of work. It was a very high-budget shoot – more like a film set than a commercial set. It ran something like thirty minutes and consequently took many days to film, with a large technical crew. The reason why I had to keep returning to the set night after night was because, as 'talent', I was basically insignificant. The real stars were the tech crew and director, who were actively collaborating and experimenting and creating and recreating the infomercial right there on the spot – editing and re-editing endlessly. They had used three child actors, who were filmed innocently running and playing inside the house, at night. The director and crew were trying to create a sense of imminent danger lurking outside the house by filming from voyeuristic camera angles etc. as though the criminal was 'out there' somewhere – in the dark, looking in, waiting to strike. In this equation I was insignificant; they could have used a wooden dummy instead. – Mark Gowers, actor*

In this way you will earn the respect of crew and director and can hope to get more work.

> The best thing about having now seen the movie is understanding the plot – I had no idea what I was doing during filming. (Ian McKellen on filming *The Hobbit: An Unexpected Journey* (Peter Jackson, 2012))[5]

> ❝*While working in the chorus and understudying Frankie Howerd at the Prince of Wales in 1966/7, I was asked to do one day's filming on* Poor Cow, *directed by Ken Loach. I agreed but did not ask permission from my boss Bernard Delfont. During the course of the day, Ken told me off for being too Frankie Howerd in one of my close-ups. Naturally, I toned it down. And he kept me so long I just made it for the quarter back in Piccadilly. A year or so later, I saw in the trailer that there was my close-up being utterly Frankie Howerd. You never know what they will choose. – John Halstead, actor*

To the tutor

How do we empower the young actor with the skills to prepare for screen work? Understanding of one's physical self is an area often ignored in screen acting classes – as though the desire to act on screen carries a built-in narcissistic confidence. For the majority of performers starting out, nothing could be further from the truth. Theatre training is very different; the emphasis is generously on both the psychological and the physical approach to character creation, which are explored over weeks of rehearsal, usually with all the actors and director present every day. Not so with film, where, especially in film school or university film departments, the emphasis is on gathering the equipment, finalizing storyboards, finding locations and props. Rehearsal itself is quite often

---

[5]'Ian McKellen on Filming the Hobbit', interview with Antonia Molloy, *The Independent*, 5 December 2014. Available at: https://www.independent.co.uk/arts-entertainment/films/news/ian-mckellen-on-filming-the-hobbit-i-had-no-idea-what-i-was-doing-9905416.html [accessed 25 July 2018].

left to the actors, and the only contact time with the director will be on the day of the shoot. We urge workshop leaders to sensitively encourage actors to accustom themselves to their appearance on screen. It is an essential tool for monitoring their own performances and moderating the level of engagement with their unseen audience. It is part of the job.

Learning to like yourself is no easy task but it is achievable. It's a question of getting used to yourself in a supportive yet artistically challenging environment, and this can be achieved with simple but effective exercises.

EXERCISE 3:1 I KNOW WHAT I LIKE

Each actor sits in a chair that has been placed in a circle with enough distance between them to avoid any sense of confinement. Dim the lighting slightly to encourage relaxation. Ask the actors to close their eyes, relax and breathe smoothly. Allow a few minutes to pass to allow the collective breathing to find its own relaxed pace. Then gently ask the students to think of someone they admire or are fond of and what it is about them they like. Each student should then, in turn, with eyes still closed, verbalize their thoughts when you touch them on the shoulder.

Almost always, each response will completely ignore any reference to physical appearance, but rather will describe an attribute of some kind – a personality trait or something positive the person has said. Rarely, if ever, in the execution of this exercise have we found that a student actor commented on the physical attributes of the person. Instinctively, they know that these are less important.

We need to remove the negative view of ourselves that we think others have of us, not just in life, but in the actor's life as played out through character from first reading to ultimate screening.

The student, having connected with this supportive environment, should now be able to repeat the exercise but this time focusing on the most *interesting* physical aspects of other people and to accept the interestingness of their own physical life.

EXERCISE 3:2 SAY AGAIN?

Actors should work in pairs (A & B) and each pair performs in turn. This is an exercise in exploring the possibilities of a text. Once every pair has performed, A and B swap roles and the exercise is repeated. Here is an example of the dialogue to be used:

A. Well?
B. I don't know.

The task is never to say 'I don't know' in the same way. At first there will be a tendency just to emphasize different words (*I* don't know, I *don't* know, I don't *know*) or to use different levels of anger or confusion. However, by considering a backstory, a previous or given circumstance, there are apparently endless ways in which these three words can be performed.

Don't rush this exercise; allow the actors time to consider these circumstances. See how many times you can go round the group without repeating a rendering of the text. As we will see in Chapter 7, listening to, and working with, your fellow actor/s is crucial and you must be sufficiently flexible to adjust your delivery of text as required.

EXERCISE 3:3 PRETEXTS FOR CHANGING SUBTEXTS

As indicated above, whilst it is imperative that the actor prepares, because of the frequent lack of rehearsal he or she may find that assumptions they had made differ from those of the director. The director has the final say: it is she who has the overall artistic vision and each actor's place within it. This exercise will help the training actors to adapt to this inevitable tyranny of the director!

Provide the actors with a script (a single page will do) that they should to learn *and rehearse* on their own prior to the session. Here is an example:

A. Have you seen my shoes?

B. Have you checked your feet?

C. Leave him/her alone.

A. Yeah, leave me alone.

B. Always expects everyone else to look after his/her stuff.

C. Where did you last have them?

B. Probably chucked them on the floor as usual.

A. Will you get off my case?

C. You should take more care. They can't have gone far.

B. Perhaps they walked off on their own.

A. You are not remotely funny you know. (pause) Hey! I am supposed to be going out. A little help would be nice.

C. Which ones are they?

A. The ones I usually wear. The black ones.

C. The ones with the worn-down heels?

A. Don't you start.

B. Why don't you wear some others?

A. They … they're in the wash.

B. What?

A. The only other ones I've got are my trainers and I put them in the wash.

C. In the washing machine?

A. Well, yeah. They were getting a bit smelly.

B. At last something we can agree on. Those black shoes are smelly too.

C. S/he's right.

A. Where are they!?

C. I put them outside.

In the workshop session they are asked to perform the scene following instructions from either the workshop leader or from a member of the group. The performing trio may have presumed (for example) that the scene takes place between a parent and two siblings. However, they may be asked to perform it as being between two parents and a child, three friends in a flat, a couple and a lodger, and so on.

What is required of the actors is that they are able to adapt quickly to the new circumstances they are presented with and be alive to the new possibilities afforded by the unexpected interpretation. Both text and subtext will need to be re-examined. Is there a history of parental favouritism at work? Are any of the flatmates in a relationship? Do they want to be? Have they been? Is there resentment about the lodger in the house? Why is s/he there? What is the nature of the relations s/he has with the others in the house? Is A forgetful? Malicious? Decisions will have to be made by the actors whatever interpretation they bring to the new given circumstances. The exercise is about reacting to the demands of the moment.

Variation. If actors in the session have been working from the same script, you can also mix the casts to provide further experience of performing with other characters with limited preparation time. The demands made by this exercise relate to many of the skills in the following chapters and could be returned to.

EXERCISE 3:4 CAN YOU TALK AND ACT AT THE SAME TIME?

For this exercise the tutor can use any short text the students have learned. They should have run the lines and be word-perfect. The tutor then asks them to play the scene whilst carrying out an activity. This will give them practice in adapting to the needs of the director, who may not want 'talking heads' dialogue.

Possible activities include: washing up, ironing, making the bed, playing a game of cards, playing table tennis, cooking a meal, watching TV, driving and so on. Figure 5 shows an actor maintaining her emotional state and control of the dialogue whilst coping with putting on a coat; the activity becomes part of the physical interpretation of the text. Draw students' attention to the way in which an activity can open up new possibilities for the text and its timing. There is also an opportunity here to impose a genre on the performance – romcom, sitcom or drama.

FIGURE 5 Exercise 3:4 Talking and acting at the same time! Photo by Abby Timms.

Screen performances to consider

It is generally accepted that the aphorism 'there are no small parts, only small actors' was coined by Constantin Stanislavski. Whether he originated the saying or not, it is worth remembering. No doubt you have observed a performance – not the starring role – that appears to leap off the screen? Sometimes it takes only minutes or even seconds for a screen career to present itself fully-formed and completely energized. We are not talking here about scene stealing; we are discussing the single act of character presentation within a small time frame that creates a stir, a memory. The actor has gone to work and done their job. And this professionalism can be the gateway to more substantial roles. This list contains not just new faces introducing themselves through sterling performances but seasoned actors taking on memorable non-lead roles.

- Lucy Liu in *Beverly Hills, 90210* (Fox, 1990–2000, Season 2, Episode 6)
- Mickey Rourke in *Body Heat* (Lawrence Kasdan, 1981)
- Johnny Depp in *A Nightmare on Elm Street* (Wes Craven, 1984)
- Cuba Gooding Jr in *Coming to America* (John Landis, 1988)
- Queen Latifah in *Jungle Fever* (Spike Lee, 1991)
- Viola Davis in *The Substance of Fire* (Daniel J. Sullivan, 1996)
- Jennifer Lawrence in *Monk* (Universal, 2002–9, Season 5, Episode 3)

> *“Turn your mic off when you go to the loo! I learned that early on when I worked in TV news. – Sarah Leigh, actor*

Screen Actors' Motto #3:
Take my tools, arrive on time, do a good job.

4 KEEPING IT REAL

That is the playground you've created, so why not stay there and play? It gets rid of that notion of playing between times, which often people talk about – waiting for the next shot. I don't buy that. Whatever you can do to give yourself a sense of continuity can only add to the work.

DANIEL DAY-LEWIS[1]

To the actor

Daniel Day-Lewis is notoriously stringent about maintaining the screen character he has carefully created. He does so throughout the entire shoot of a film, both on and off the set. Most actors will break between the calls of 'Cut!' and 'Action!' but he continues to 'live' the character. Not every actor can do that, not every actor wants to do that and not every actor needs to do that. For him, that approach works. He views the process in its entirety, from first impressions on reading the script to the final call of 'It's a WRAP!'

Like many screen actors, Day-Lewis has developed a methodology for sustaining character consistency throughout the various technical challenges of shooting a film. Impressive when you consider that most professional filmmakers shoot around five or six pages of script on a typical day, which equates to roughly five minutes of film. To get there, the process will include innumerable starts and stops. In essence, Daniel

---

[1]'How Daniel Day-Lewis' Notoriously Rigorous Role Preparation Has Yielded Another Oscar Contender', interview with Chris Sullivan, *The Independent*, 1 February 2008. Available at: https://www.independent.co.uk/arts-entertainment/films/features/how-daniel-day-lewis-notoriously-rigorous-role-preparation-has-yielded-another-oscar-contender-776563.html [accessed 11 August 2018].

Day-Lewis' developed methodology allows him personal space to maintain a sense of 'keeping it real'.

In performance terms this means showing who the character is through an honest, considered and maintained truthfulness take after take. You may feel that the very nature of filmmaking disrupts 'truthfulness' because of the technical requirements. And you would be right, it does. One element of the process is trying to capture a performance and the other is trying to deliver it. Two artistic ends negotiating a notoriously erratic middle and each frustrated by scheduled and unscheduled periods of inaction. The actor can be stopped literally mid-sentence whilst delivering the most powerful of speeches because a boom mic has slipped into shot. Or during an intimate or confrontational moment, requiring the performers to stay in close and uncomfortable proximity as another take is set up. Everybody and everything on the work floor can become a distraction.

Your mission, should you choose to accept it, is to carry on acting. That is, once they have replaced the burned-out fuse or fed the alligator you have to wrestle in scene 19 – don't worry, they will have plenty of spare fuses. Of course, it would be convenient for a screen actor to simply pick up a script, get into character and act, following the dramatic arc in neat chronological order from page one through to the end. Unfortunately, in film it doesn't happen that way. In theatre it does – plays happen in real time, though the story doesn't have to. With character construction and delivery, you may feel the stage actor has a distinctly unfair advantage over the screen actor. Their work during a performance is uninterrupted. All the character development, script changes, motivations are catered for during the rehearsal period in preparation for direct communication with a live audience.

The luxury of performing in a single place on a single day is rarely afforded the actor in the medium of film. Whilst the stage actor is creating their work in a rehearsal room, for the film actor this usually takes place at home and she will have to wait months to see the results of her efforts. Not all films experience extreme delays but from the moment a performance is captured on film to its public release can take a long time: particularly films where special effects/CGI play a big part.

Filmmaking is a highly technical process and by its very nature demands of the actor energy, attentiveness, discipline, commitment, flexibility. Say it again: 'Film making is a highly technical process and by its very nature demands of the actor; energy, attentiveness, discipline, commitment, flexibility.' Repeat it again but this time whilst riding a bicycle … ah, that's exactly what I want … what's that? … the light was wrong? … let's do it again … what? Make-up needs a dab … continuity, can you please check, was he wearing cycle clips in the last shot? … and, Action! … agghhhh! where has the sun gone? … Cut!

There will always be distractions. How do you marry coping with these to your desire to play the character 'correctly', to deliver the lines as written and keep your face in the directed pose? Oh, and how about at the same time managing a character's driven and directed activity whilst clinging to your backstory. Or maybe you're manipulating some forceps whilst performing open-heart surgery and delivering a line such as: 'Pericarditis has thinned the membranes and they have become irritated and inflamed. Quick! Wheel in the electronic myocardial infarction deflector!' All without bumping into the furniture or tripping over the lighting cables. Talk about distractions!

- The screen actor's performance at the shooting stage is fragmentary.
- The breaks in line/character delivery can be both intentional and unintentional.
- The calls of 'Cut!' can come fast and frequently due to the director's vision of a scene, how they want it to look, feel and sound …
- Or because of some issue that presents itself randomly.

It's all part of the filmmaking process. The screen actor is at the untender mercy of the technical complexities of the medium. What can you do but concentrate?

Interruptions! Interruptions! Interruptions!

A complete and uninterrupted screen performance is almost impossible to give on a film set. Everything is shot in carefully designed pieces and will only make storytelling sense once they are stitched together through the editing process. Add to that the necessity of non-sequential shooting (see Chapter 8) and you may wonder how film actors ever get to complete a fully rounded character on the screen. But they do: performances are created and maintained amidst the unexpected, sometimes adding a new and exciting energy to the actors working together in a scene as they cope with the same experience at the same time. This aspect of acting vs the technical creates a camaraderie that may seem alien to most professions. The collation of fractured scenes and the process of achieving them adds an appreciation of each other's plight and artistic struggle. The communal, concentrated focus is on getting the best from each other.

Distractions come in different guises. The actor may wish for a zen-like atmosphere in order to conjure up the character, but wishes for artistic solitude very rarely come to fruition. They might do in the movies but not on an industrial and busy film set. Before you continue reading, have a listen. From where you are located what can *you* hear? Cars passing, an airplane above, a helicopter, voices discussing something, voices arguing about something, birds squawking, the rustling of leaves, rain falling, the buzzing of a fly, an ambulance siren, police siren, a breeze blowing, thunder, radio, television, somebody sneezing, coughing, a baby crying, laughter, dogs barking, a cat meowing, a mobile phone ringing, bathroom flushing, the hum of a refrigerator, somebody knocking on a door, an ice-cream van belting out an awful organ-grinding version of 'I'm Forever Blowing Bubbles'? You get the aural picture. Chances are that you will have heard or are hearing one of the above as you read this. More than likely, you are hearing several at the same time. In real life we very rarely experience complete and uninterrupted silence. Even if you immerse your head in water whilst taking a bath, you will hear your heart beating. (If you don't, then it may be in your best interests to come up for air. Like, *now!*) Intrusive sounds that interfere with filming are even harder to escape. A purpose-built film studio may block out the exterior cacophony, but what if you are shooting outside the protected environment? Or inside a location that has no soundproofing?

There are other trespassing culprits besides sound. Electrical issues are well known for their temperamental timing. Generators can blow. Bulbs can crack. And there are others lurking. Set-dressings can fall. Props discovered that are out of continuity sync. Camera placement problems. Interference from electronic gadgets (it's not *your* phone, is it?). Sightline problems. A supporting artist, daydreaming (or perhaps seeking a nanosecond of fame), staring into the lens of the camera. Has there ever been a film shoot where everything has gone according to plan? No.

All of these can be hostile to your objective as an actor to contribute to the creation of a dramatic paradigm and to serve the story. With that in mind, it is worth noting that not all interruptions are technical. The actor you are playing opposite may dry (forget their lines). There will be days when *you* dry, or one of your fellow actors is not feeling their best. Everybody has days like that. With all the possible breaks in performance, how do you keep it real?

The bad news is that there isn't one single methodology. Like Daniel Day-Lewis or the actor sitting opposite you in a scene, you will have to develop your own flexible tactics. The good news is that devotion of time and consideration will assist you towards experimenting with various coping mechanisms, all of which will be based in concentration. And it is this concentration that will guide your performance back onto a delivery plane when an interruption has broken the flow. It may seem obvious but when something goes awry, stay focused. It's not in your or the film's interest to huff, puff and get angry. It is your job to remain alert, helpful and ready to begin the scene again. The world you create for your character is a real world – *for them*. Aggravating incidents may seem purposely designed to stem the flow of your engagement with the moment. Protection of *the moment* is something you will learn to control by cultivating an ability to switch your performance on *and* off as required. Or rather, it is like pressing 'pause': the emotional pitch, the physicality, the vocal life remain suspended until the record button – 'Action!' – is pressed. Everybody on a set has to constantly adjust and readjust. Keep in your headspace and don't get distracted.

So, amongst the possible interruptions, how do you manoeuvre towards keeping it real?

Concentration

- Concentration involves focusing on something you are doing.
- Utilizing it requires developing the ability to deflect intrusion.
- It will empower you to separate your job from other people's as you all work towards the same outcome.
- It is something that is central to all performance, no matter the chosen medium.

Concentration is a revitalization pit stop. It allows you stop, think, plan and advance, no matter how irritating the interruption, whilst the 'pause' button is holding your performance in suspension.

- Concentration links directly to imagination.
- Imagination is a place we can retreat to during interruptions.
- The pit stop is where we can psychologically refill with images, feelings and motivations all directly linked to our character.
- Focusing on the backstory will assist our understanding of our character and will help guide us back into the drama after yet another break in 'the moment'.
- In the character's world, relationships, desires, goals, obstacles and outcomes are organic. The lights and cables are artificial. Ignore them, but don't trip over them!

> Without extremely developed powers of concentration, nothing you do as an actor will have much substance.[2]

You don't need complete silence in order to concentrate. It is a matter of managing the incoming distractions. Avoid unnecessary conversations. The director or the actor(s) you are about to do the scene with are the obvious exceptions to this. At such times, there are two people in your head – you and the character. The character waits for the call to come forward: you the actor listen to any instructions and calmly indicate you have understood, feeding this new information to the waiting character in your head. Chatty or nervous people can unintentionally drain energy and that will bring on a lapse in *your* concentration, not theirs. You don't have to be rude to anybody, but it is important that you protect your time. Your time is your character's time. Conversations about the weather, politics, your next audition, the director's dress sense can be saved for after work.

All actors are different. Each has an individual approach to concentration. There is no 'right' way, no industry standard. During a long hiatus, perhaps whilst waiting for the next shot or take to be set up:

[2]'Concentration for Actors', TheatreGroup.com. Available at: http://www.theatrgroup.com/Method/actor_concentration.html [accessed 20 May 2019].

- Some need to leave the set between takes and maintain character through quiet solitude.
- Some will walk around the periphery of the set quietly reciting dialogue yet to be shot or reshot.
- Some will listen to music through headphones.
- Some will find a comfortable chair and have a snooze.
- Some will use the time between takes to read a book.
- Some will use the time between takes to write a book.

What supports actors through the various approaches is their craft, and part of that is noting the importance of backstory preparation (Chapter 2). Your character *lives* on the set – not the crew, not the director. That is not arrogance, that is imagination. The more you imagine something is yours – the room, the relationship, the street, the story etc. – the more you will strengthen your concentration. In this way, after the call of 'Cut!', two actors together will find the restarting point in their characters' relationship as soon as 'Action!' is called again. This has to be achieved irrespective of their individual methodology. Ownership (or, if you like, knowledge) will point you towards regaining a natural flow every time it is required. After every start and stop. No matter how many.

Patience

Let's take a break here, relax and spare a thought for performers as human cogs within the cinematic machinery who had to withstand particularly extreme challenges. Virginia Cherrill had to endure a scene in *City Lights* (1931) that took over 300 takes in order to satisfy director Charlie Chaplin's unshakeable vision of how it should look. Tom Cruise was required to walk through a door and down a hallway for a scene in the film *Eyes Wide Shut*. Simple? Not through the lens of the director Stanley Kubrick's camera. He was looking for 'something' within that assumed simplicity. Tom Cruise had to do sixty-nine takes before Kubrick was satisfied with the authenticity of the scene as he saw it.

Each time you begin to record a scene again, it must appear that the lines or action you are delivering are being presented for the very first time, every time. For actors, spontaneity is a calculated act of delivery.

When an audience sees the finished film, they will not be aware – nor should they be – of any of the technical hitches that the actor has endured in order to bring the character to cinematic life. Technical problems and interruptions are part of the job, your job. Be patient with them. It's all part of the filmmaking DNA.

> Film acting is incredibly tedious, just by its nature. It's incredibly, mind numbingly slow. (Hugh Grant)[3]

It may be worth stating the obvious here; filmmaking is not a clock-in/clock-out occupation. On a film set you can relinquish any expectations of working regular nine-to-five hours. You won't be able to leave the set early because it's your uncle's birthday or because you are going on an important date or have to take your budgie to the vet. Not a chance. Accepting that reality will allow you to progress with a positive and implicit obligation to the filmmaking process.

Break over.

'Keeping it real' necessitates you look after you. Control what is within your domain. Let the director take care of the actor who is desperately trying to remember lines. When problems on a set are identified, they are fixed as quickly as possible. And be kind to the co-performer experiencing a problem – on another day it could be you. The common understanding on a set can be summed up as follows:

- Everybody working on a film wants the very best for that film.
- Interruptions for you are interruptions for everybody.
- Everybody has to cope.
- As an actor, like every other member of the team in their particular department, you will have to handle each and every situation as they arise.
- Delays will cost valuable and expensive shooting time, which will require you to stay on site, ready to be called once the problem has been identified and amended.

[3]Quoted on BrainyQuote.com. Available at: https://www.brainyquote.com/quotes/keywords/film_acting.html [accessed 22 November 2018].

Teamwork

These commonalities create a thinking, problem-solving bond between cast and crew. Each side supports the other, especially through the frustrating times. And even they won't last for ever. If they did, no film would ever get made.

All on-set disruption must be viewed as temporary. This part of the filmmaking process cannot afford the actor the luxury of sitting back and saying, well, I was ready to give my all, but hey, the moment has gone now: your career may also be gone if you adopt that attitude! Screen actors accept that their performances are subject to the unpredictable whim of the technical. They always were and always will be. In this unique occupational hazard, you are not alone. The same problems arise for all film actors, be they Robert De Niro, Dame Judi Dench, Meryl Streep, Idris Elba or your favourite player in your favourite television series.

Thankfully, the actor does not have to resolve technical interruptions. That is the job of the sound recordist if it involves sound, or the cameraperson if it involves the camera. Likewise, a dozen or more other departmentalized contributors should they be at fault. In polite terminology – mind your own business! Look after your own work, as any 'suggestions' from you, even acting ones, may not be received kindly. Acting (or, more accurately, *your* acting) is *your* responsibility as part of the team. If an intrusive sound like a sonorous wasp or a dive-bombing bluebottle is jeopardizing the recording of your performance, then the director will naturally call 'Cut!' And when you hear that three-letter word, don't take it personally. Remember, most sudden stoppages may have absolutely nothing to do with your performance. If they do, then the director will quietly (hopefully) speak to you and the other performers within the scene to resolve any actor issues that have arisen. Don't confuse direction with criticism. You have your job. The director has theirs. As the protagonist in *The Godfather* says: 'It's not personal. It's strictly business.' Your responsibility, when interruptions present themselves, is to maintain intensity, subtlety and creativity – repeatedly. A delay may be only minutes long or sometimes many hours. A major technical problem may even necessitate an end to that day's shoot, with a call for early the next morning to continue with the scene (pick-up). Be ready for it!

To the tutor

The novice screen actor 'keeping it real' may very easily be overwhelmed by the technical requirements the process demands. Finding ways to create and maintain an understanding of character is important. Self, and peer, evaluation of the student actor's inventions will help influence their approach to screen performance, current and future. The foundation block that actors require to harvest complete ownership of character is imagination. Maintaining it requires concentration. These are indispensable tools. And they need practice.

> Creating imaginatively is what acting is about. (Stella Adler, quoted in Kissel 2000: 73)

Note: Notions of concentration and coping with disruptions are magnified when the screen performance involves a mixture of studio and location shots perhaps spread over weeks or months. Special attention is given to these challenges in Chapter 8.

EXERCISE 4:1 FACE-OFF

This exercise is developed from the well-known 'hot-seating' exercise that allows fellow actors to question each other to deepen the knowledge of a character (see Chapter 2). Present the actor with a photograph of someone they don't know. A cutting from a magazine or newspaper will suffice, but don't use celebrities. Give them five minutes to make some instant decisions about the person in the photograph – and an instant backstory. The actor is then asked questions by the group, individually and in turn, to which he or she has to respond immediately and 'truthfully'. In this version the camera shoots a close-up of the actor's face as he or she is being questioned. Recording the exercise will allow the actor and the group to review the minutiae of facial responses that accompany the verbal responses and analyse the actor's ability to concentrate on the situation whilst responding.

EXERCISE 4:2 HOOK UP, MAKE UP, BREAK UP

In this exercise students must struggle against the tendency to fall into stereotypes. There should be no stock characters or responses. Find the child – remember how it was to play, to pick and put down emotions and actions at the drop of a hat. Working in pairs, students are required to use this apparently bland dialogue to tell the story of a whole relationship:

A. I love you.
B. I love you too.

The actors may decide when to reverse the order of lines but should not introduce any new dialogue as they improvise the following scenarios:

1 The first time these words are said. Then:
2 After first intimacy.
3 'You make me laugh.'
4 'I need you to believe me.'
5 At the altar.
6 'I'm off to work – see you later.'
7 After a row.
8 Making up after an affair.
9 'I'm just saying this. I want it to be true.'
10 'I forgive you.'
11 Leaving.

After each exchange the actors should turn away from one another, take a moment and then face each other again. In Figure 6 we see four samples from this 'narrative'. In the first the actors are saying 'I love you' for the first time. In the second these words have become a routine exchange. The third follows an argument and in the final version they are at the point of splitting up.

FIGURE 6 Exercise 4:2 Hook up, make up, break up. Photo by Abby Timms.

Variation for larger groups. In pairs prepare ONE of the above versions of the text and play them in sequence. Try changing the sequence. The camera should pan from pair to pair.

Discuss to what extent the actors were able to respond to the actual situation presented by their fellow actor. Were they able to escape the obvious? Were they able to concentrate and maintain character and emotional context?

It is a cliché that 'the eyes are the windows of the soul'. It is also a truth that we all recognize. If lying or trying to hide how we are feeling, we will often avoid eye contact. Paradoxically, if trying to convince somebody (even if we *are* lying), we will look directly into his or her eyes. We are instinctively aware of the transparency of our emotions that our eyes will transmit. Looking straight into somebody's eyes is a very intimate form of contact that can convey both positive (love, honesty) and negative (aggression, challenge) emotions. We have often observed that screen actors, aware of this, will tend to hide their eyes at moments of high drama. This *may* be a truthful response, but it also may be the actor avoiding the invasion of the audience or, in this case, the camera. It is useful to employ strategies to find alternatives to hiding the eyes – unless there is an artistic reason for so doing. (For example, it may be important that the spectator is left unclear at this point in the story.) If the actor is responding to a situation alone in a room, there will be little excuse for hiding the reaction. When playing with others, the requirements are more nuanced. Consider this dialogue, which could be taken from any soap or romantic film:

EXERCISE 4:3 LOOK AT ME WHEN YOU'RE IGNORING ME!

A. I love you.
B. I know.
A. Do you love me too?
B. Of course. Of course I do.

As we have already discussed, there are many ways of playing such a scene depending on the characters, their backstory, the storyline and the immediate situation. Let us assume that A really means it and that his/her objective is to get confirmation that the love is returned. B is having doubts but has the objective of not wanting to hurt A's feelings. One way to show this ambivalence is for B to avoid eye contact when responding. But wouldn't A pick up on this signal? Wouldn't B be forced to engage in eye contact (and then perhaps offer that second 'of course I do')? In Figure 7 the man is hoping to see such affirmation, but her 'of course I do' signals to the viewing audience that she is being evasive.

FIGURE 7 Exercise 4:3 Look at me when you're ignoring me! Photo by Abby Timms.

How long could s/he hold such a look before having to turn away? Or would B avoid the eye contact by closing his or her eyes and moving in for a kiss, thus giving a strong signal of love whilst hiding the betrayal emanating from the eyes? Together with the director, the screen actor has to decide what they want the viewer to take from the scene. Are these characters genuinely in love? If not, then who is fooling whom? Eye contact – or not – will be a key component of how this scene reads. Shielding, or in other ways hiding the eyes, can be part of this, and a useful exercise is to ask training screen actors to perform this scene in a variety of ways. Review the footage and see whether the intentions and objectives of the performance have been reflected in what appears on the screen. Discuss how the actor can let the viewer know that s/he is lying whilst also convincing us that the other character will believe the lie?

EXERCISE 4:4 HERE'S LOOKING AT YOU, KID

Two actors sit facing each other at a distance of a metre or two holding a blank piece of card so as to mask the lower part of the face. Only the eyes and eyebrows are visible. The actors should not plan any action but merely react in silence to what they perceive they receive. What happens is highly unpredictable and can be very intense. Exaggerated expressions will quickly be exposed as false. It may be that initially nothing appears to happen but sooner or later perhaps...

A. Thinks he observes a quizzical narrowing of the eyebrows. He returns this perceived look by a miniscule raising of his own eyebrows.

B. (Who may not be aware of having given any signals) reads and receives this sign and responds, perhaps with amusement.

A. (Who sees only the eyes and not any accompanying smile) may read in the eyes and the temples an invitation which she may decide to return or reject.

B. If 'rejected' the eyes may express disappointment, despair, lack of concern, *pretended* lack of concern and so on.

Allow the 'conversation' to run as long as is productive or until the actors get tired of holding the cardboard! A third actor, C, could be involved to give an additional dynamic to the exchange opening the improvisation to possibilities of jealousy, deceit, guilt, a need for approval and so forth. Then review the material, comparing what the actors believed was being communicated to what is being read on screen by the viewers. Note especially those moments when the acting becomes demonstrated and 'shown'.

Variations on Exercise 4:4

- You can try giving the actors clear roles: parent/child; boss/employee; divorcing couple; first date.
- Give a location: On a train; a social gathering; during a business meeting.

- A hospital drama. Shades of *Grey's Anatomy*. Get hold of some medical masks and improvise a surgical operation using cutlery. Explore concern, hesitation, confidence, panic, flirting.
- Or develop it into an 'emotions' game where an actor is given an emotion to communicate using only the eyes. Shooting in close-up would be advantageous. The actor will find that the tighter the shot, the less they have to do; the more they have to think and 'live through'.

Screen performances to consider

It's not always comfortable being a screen actor, but you are there to do a job. Consider Charles Laughton's role in the Hollywood epic *The Hunchback of Notre Dame* (William Dieterle, 1939). The actor appears as the tormented Quasimodo, aided by the ingenious make-up skills of Perc Westmore, whose job it was to bury Laughton under pounds of rubber. Laughton in return somehow manages to 'keep it real' and unremittingly engages us with the humanity of the character. Every morning of the shoot, beginning promptly at four a.m., Laughton would sit in the make-up chair for two and a half hours. His face was gradually distorted by the careful layering of a special rubber application, along with the addition of a protruding eye. The hunched back consisted of a specially constructed framework weighing four pounds. To play the character realistically, the actor requested that his ears were plugged so that he couldn't react to any unscheduled and unexpected sounds. Add to this a shooting schedule that coincided with 100-degree summer heat and you have the makings of a very uncomfortable experience. Laughton gives a masterclass in ownership of both character and circumstances – without the aid of CGI.

Likewise, we invite you to consider John Hurt's performance as John Merrick in *The Elephant Man* (David Lynch, 1980). It is intriguing to watch and feel how the emotional dynamic of his acting draws the viewer in. Hurt underwent nine hours of daily prosthetic application to become the character – and no CGI here either.

Screen Actors' Motto #4:
Acting is a world of make-believe – so make us believe it.

5 THIS HAS NEVER HAPPENED TO ME BEFORE

To the actor

The cinema is truth twenty-four times per second, and every cut is a lie.

JEAN-LUC GODARD, *LE PETIT SOLDAT*, 1960

For most of our lives we do not know what is going to happen next. Looking back we can see the patterns that shaped the events of our personal and working lives, but *in the moment* every second is presented to us to deal with as it occurs. *How* we deal with it will depend on the circumstances we were in at that time. A friend calls out of the blue. Our response will depend upon what we are doing and feeling at the time. It may also be affected by the nature of our relationship with the friend. If we are busy, we may want to put them off until another time. Their reason for calling may override this, or may irritate us further with its triviality. The possibilities are endless. Each second of the conversation presents us with new decisions to make in the light of what we hear and against the background of the past relationship and immediate personal circumstances. The importance of having created this backstory is dealt with in Chapter 2. In this chapter we will consider ways of developing your ability to act as if you do not know what is going to happen.

> I think on some level, you do your best things when you're a little off-balance, a little scared. You've got to work from mystery, from wonder, from not knowing. (Willem Dafoe)[1]

Of course, one would hope that you do know what is going to happen. In your research and preparation, you will have at least read the script through to the end! Your backstory must fit in with the demands of the screenplay, however creatively. The job of the screen actor is to present authentic responses to the forensic eye of the camera lens, and any anticipation will destroy this authenticity. Not all directors work this way. Mike Leigh, for example, through improvisation and luxuriously profound character preparation time, habitually withholds information from the actors in order to achieve a totally truthful response in the moment. It is said that none of the characters in *Vera Drake* (2004) were aware of the dénouement until the police came to arrest Vera.[2] But this is a very particular way of working and for most screen actors it remains central to your preparation that you have a sense of your superobjective that takes into account all the information that can be gleaned from the screenplay. (See Chapter 8: Where were we?) This fictive backstory will provide the impetus for responding to other characters and situations *as if for the first time* – even on the eighth take!

Superobjective. If 'objectives' are about the step-by-step ways we use to pursue our character's motivations, the superobjective involves standing back and looking over the trajectory of the whole course of the action. This doesn't mean playing the beginning as if you know how it all ends! The purpose of defining for yourself your superobjective is to ensure that each motivation and objective you pursue has a coherence when the final dénouement is played. It is about knowing the journey you are on.

---

[1] 'Willem Dafoe: "You do your best work when you're scared"', interview with Steve Rose, *The Guardian*, 4 July 2012. Available at: https://www.theguardian.com/film/2012/jul/04/willem-defoe-hunter-interview [accessed 25 July 2018].

[2] 'Vera Drake – Mike Leigh Q&A', compiled by Jack Foley, IndieLondon.co.uk. Available at: http://www.indielondon.co.uk/film/vera_drake_leighQ&A.html [accessed 20 May 2019].

In creating your backstory you will have researched everything there is to know about your character. Also, you will have had to identify what it is that you *don't* know and which you need to invent. From your theatre acting you will be well versed in identifying objectives and superobjective and, for a particular scene, to know what your character is bringing onto the stage in terms of previous circumstances and immediate given circumstances.

Immediate Circumstances. There are occasions, especially when moving between locations and where there is also a time gap (see Chapter 8), that particular immediate events need to be recalled. You are gasping for air as your damaged spacesuit gives way during your spacewalk: cut to the safety of the airlock and you must bring those immediate circumstances with you.

You will know why your character is there and what they want. In theatre this period of discovery is embedded in the rehearsal process where, under the stewardship of the director, relationships will be evolved, questions answered, contradictions explored and the character's psychology deepened. The screen actor generally does not have this luxury. Many screen actors will find that rehearsals are only used for establishing blocking and enabling the director and crew to make decisions about the number of shots and angles and the requirements for lighting. You may not meet your fellow actors until the day of the shoot. Screen actors are much less supported in their craft and the expectations heaped upon them are far greater. They are expected to turn up, fully prepared, whilst not knowing what is going to happen.

> Act before you think – your instincts are more honest than your thoughts. (Sanford Meisner)[3]

[3]Quoted on AZQuotes.com. Available at: https://www.azquotes.com/quote/532591 [accessed 25 July 2018].

Anticipation

Avoiding anticipation is crucial to all acting. It is perhaps one of the most blatant errors in poorly rehearsed or directed theatre, as the recipient of a line or an event will start to respond to what they do not yet know. They 'telegraph' their reaction even before the telegram has arrived. The eye of the camera is even less forgiving than the theatre audience and any such counterfeit response will be obvious. For this reason, such errors are comparatively rare on screen as the editor and director will work hard to eliminate any examples that have survived the shoot. They are still to be found, though, especially in productions created under the pressure of tight schedules. A few minutes viewing of soap operas will provide examples. This chapter is devoted to exercises that help screen actors develop the skill of working moment to moment: it has never happened to you before.

Consider the following scenario. A woman comes home from work. Is she tired? Has she had a good day? She pours two glasses of wine and sits down with the post. She opens it. She starts to read it, reacts, and then checks the envelope. It is addressed to her husband. She reacts to her mistake and is about to put the letter back in the envelope but then decides to read it. We see it is a credit card bill. She is troubled. The key turns in the door. Her husband is home. He calls out cheerfully and then enters the room.

- This scene, perhaps lasting half a minute on screen, contains many points where decisions have to be made and where you need to train yourself to 'not know' what will happen next. There are also moments of 'knowing' which help to set the scene. She 'knows' that her husband arrives home about the same time and so prepares a drink for both of them. She, and we, assume that the relationship is strong because of this anticipation of the other's needs and the relaxed manner in which the wife settles down to domesticity. The actor then has to make a series of decisions:
- What am I expecting from the post?
- Do bills frighten me?
- Why does she accidentally open the bill addressed to her husband?
- Is there any suspicion there?

- Is it an accident? Thoughtlessness?
- Has this happened before?
- Does he get irritated or even angry if she opens his post?
- Why does she decide to read it?
- Suspicion? Curiosity?
- Does something in the letter catch her eye, overriding her instinct to put the letter back in its envelope?

Then we hear the sound of her husband returning:

- Does she try to hide the letter?
- Pretend to be in the act of opening it for the first time?
- Does she hold it openly in her hand? Place it on the table?

The husband enters. What signals is she presenting?

- Is she feeling guilty? Angry? Betrayed?
- Can she make eye contact?
- Does she try to hide all emotion and behave as if nothing had happened?
- Does she succeed?

The husband has similar decisions to make. On arriving home, he has no reason to suspect that anything is wrong:

- What sort of day has he had at work?
- What emotional state is he bringing into the scene?

There is no such thing as entering 'neutrally'; his entrance too is dictated by previous circumstance. Depending on what decisions have been made by his co-performer, he will have to respond, *not* to what he knows as an actor who has read the whole script, but as the person living through this situation.

- If the bill remains hidden, will he pick up on her mood?
- Will he realize what has happened?
- Will he feel guilt? Anger? Betrayal?

- Which emotions will thread their way through the ensuing dialogue?

Or does the director say 'Cut!' and the scene ends without a word being said?

Once the second actor enters, of course, you have to remember that the scene is not just about you (see Chapter 7). The two characters (who are, after all, husband and wife and thus will be very familiar with each other's emotional 'tells') must respond to what they are being given. You cannot play your own preferred emotional through-line and ignore the situation that is being given in the moment by the other actor. The husband may, for example, see the letter, decide momentarily on defensive anger but, seeing the concern and sense of betrayal in his wife's eyes, change tack. His tense posture might collapse into an aspect of submission. Or, he may totally miss the signals from his wife, take a sip of wine and for a moment appear relaxed and content. In response she may have to clarify her state of mind through a gesture, a sound, a look. If she has decided to try to ignore the situation for the moment, he may need to pick up on some slight signal from her in order for the scene to progress. The permutations are manifold. But at each moment the screen actor must respond truthfully, from the character base, to what is there and not bring to the scene solely decisions made off camera and alone. It takes practice to be natural. As Glenda Jackson points out:

> Acting is not about dressing up. Acting is about stripping bare. The whole essence of learning lines is to forget them so you can make them sound like you thought of them that instant.[4]

To the tutor

These exercises are designed to allow and encourage the student actor to practise being 'in the moment', avoiding any traces of anticipation whilst working from their backstory, given and immediate circumstances.

---

[4]*Sunday Telegraph*, 26 July 1992. Quoted on BrainyQuote.com. Available at: https://www.brainyquote.com/quotes/glenda_jackson_368488 [accessed 25 July 2018].

EXERCISE 5:1 THE CONFRONTATION

The actor is seated. Out of shot (OOV) the text is improvised by the tutor or a fellow student. The camera remains on the seated actor. The camera operator can zoom between a full-length shot, close-up and extreme close-up (in moderation) in order to allow discussion of a range of acting responses.

The seated actor is instructed to say nothing. They are given no information about the situation or their relationship with the speaker. Their job is to listen and respond in the moment (Figure 8). They should keep as still as is naturally possible, though they may look at the speaker *once* at a moment of their choice.

FIGURE 8 Exercise 5:1 The confrontation. Photo by Abby Timms.

The off-camera speaker improvises the text. Ideally, he or she should be to the side and slightly behind the actor to avoid casual visual interaction. That single look will thus become more significant and be the result of a decision made by the actor. There can be as many pauses as feels right. The actor listens. Here is an example:

> So what happened? ... I waited for nearly two hours ... I thought we were friends ... You knew I didn't have money for a taxi ... You're so selfish sometimes ... Do you care about anybody but yourself? ...

> Aren't you going to say anything? … One minute you were there and then I suppose you got off with someone? … We said we'd stick together. Anything could have happened to you for all I knew … And anything could have happened to me on my own … Walking back in the dark … I was scared out of my wits … Not that you care … Well, I hope they were worth it, 'cause you've lost a good mate … I've always been a good mate to you, haven't I? … You make me sick … You can't even be bothered to apologize.

The speaker can mould the content in light of the responses from the silent actor. The seated actor cannot plan their responses nor anticipate the information in the text because they have never heard it before. Instead, they have to make sense of the information as it comes from the improviser and create their own understanding of the events. The actor will soon work out (in the example above) the story behind the 'conversation'. Then comes the accusation that she abandoned her friend for 'some bloke'. Is this true? Is this accusation hurtful? What was the real reason they got separated? Why doesn't she interrupt this accusation? Shame? Anger? To keep a confidence? What is it that the improviser says that makes her use the precious moment of eye contact? What will this convey? The viewers of the exercise *as presented on screen* will certainly be interpreting this look and all other aspects of her reactions.

Stripped of the ability to plan reactions and rehearse emotions, many actors new to screen work will present a surprising level of truthfulness in their performance. Here they have no choice but to be in the moment with sincerity. They are also learning the importance of listening and responding. Observers of this exercise (and as always it is important that they observe the screen not the live performance, otherwise they can get distracted from the silent actor to the improviser) will be able to provide feedback on the emotional truth of the performance and to identify where reactions could be further modulated. What did the observers presume was going on in the mind of the actor? How does this match what the actor thought they were experiencing? – for this exercise is about experiencing not performing.

EXERCISE 5:2 THE LETTER

The following exercise is designed to help the screen actor acknowledge the fact that they bring a state of mind with them into the shoot (the previous and given circumstances) and that they then have to respond, moment to moment, to events that occur during the scene. It also helps various technical aspects of performance, such as finding their mark and utilizing eyelines (see Chapter 9). The spectators should only watch the screen.

The actor is directed to enter the space, pick up a letter from the floor, take it to a table and sit down to read it (Figure 9). On the envelope is written a clue as to the sender of the letter – 'from the bank', 'from a friend', 'handwritten but unknown', 'private and confidential', 'junk mail', etc. The letter itself contains a further emotional trigger – 'good news', 'a refund', 'a legacy', 'bad news', 'a threat', 'indifferent news', 'something that irritates', 'something that pleases'. Alternatively, you, the tutor, or others in the group can write and address the letters in full, depending on how far you wish to test the actors' powers of imagination. Needless to say, it may be useful if the two triggers (the source of the letter and the contents) offer a contrast in emotions. Good news from the bank, or a letter from a partner that turns out to be a 'Dear John' letter rather than a love letter.

FIGURE 9 Exercise 5:2 The letter. Photo by Abby Timms.

The camera can pan with the actor into the room, follow the picking up of the letter and focus on the initial response of the recipient. It then pans with the actor across to the table and employs a variety of close-ups that capture their subsequent responses. Here is an example:

The actor enters. What is their mood at this point? Where have they come from? If from outside, what is the weather like? Are they expecting others to be in the room? Are they expecting mail? They pick up the letter and look at it. It is (for example) a rather official-looking letter. The trigger on the envelope says 'from a firm of solicitors'. What is the reaction to this? She crosses to the table still staring at the letter. She places her bag on the table (attention to the needs of the camera here – take care not to block what the camera may want to see!) and sits (ensuring that her chair is on its mark). She opens the letter. How does she feel? What is she expecting? The second trigger inside the letter informs her that a beloved aunt has died. Reaction to this? Why didn't she know? Guilt about not having seen her for ages? Why wasn't she invited to the funeral? She is mentioned in the will and needs to contact the office for details. Reaction to this? How does the reaction to the death combine with the news of the inheritance? The actor may consider phoning the office now. Maybe it is too late in the day. She may glance up at the wall clock momentarily (eyeline – see Chapter 9). Try letting the scene run for another thirty seconds, only ending when the director says 'Cut!' She will then have to wrestle with conflicting emotions for some time. It is often in this hiatus, where the 'action' has finished, that the acting can be at its deepest and most powerful.

An exercise such as this throws up several issues for the training screen actor to consider. The initial tendency will often be to play the scene for all it is worth. With no text to hide behind, the silence may be filled with grunts of confusion, despair or joy which, when viewed back, will expose themselves as being false and exaggerated.

A question that will be worth exploring with training screen actors is that of the nature of on-screen 'truth'. Ask your workshop group if they think they would behave the same if truly the subject of the 'confrontation' (Exercise 5:1), or alone in a room reading a letter (Exercise 5:2), as they would if another were present, or if they knew they were being watched. Truthfully, to what extent do we externalize our emotions when alone? And what is appropriate for the art of screen acting?

EXERCISE 5:3 LEARNING TO DRINK

This similar solitary exercise allows students to practise the idea that no experience has ever happened in the same way before, and continues to explore the question of the truthfulness of behaviour on screen.

The actor is presented with a cup of water and will be told what drink it represents. They will then have to drink it. The actor can decide on the previous immediate circumstance they are bringing to the scene. The camera should focus on the face of the actor, whilst the rest of the group watch the action on screen.

The actor knows that the water he is about to drink is a cocktail, a shot, a beer, coffee, tea, home-made wine, fizzy drink, water, juice, etc. He has decided whether he is thirsty, whether he likes the drink, whether he is familiar with the taste or whether he is suspicious of it. The actor's own emotion memory will help shape his first approach to the drink. (We have yet to see an actor who does not pick up hot soup or hot chocolate by holding the cup between both hands!) The way in which someone sips a cup of tea or a beer can tell us a great deal about the character and his environment. Drinking water after a period of exercise will be different from casually sipping water with a meal.

Where this exercise can be used to develop the skill of 'not anticipating' is in the trigger which the tutor (or another student) can introduce at the moment of drinking. The hot chocolate which turns out to be tepid, the tea which has too much or too little sugar, the home-made wine which tastes disgusting but you don't want to upset the aunt who made it, the coffee which is just too hot to drink, the cocktail you thought you wouldn't like but is actually quite pleasant. Again, the question arises as to whether our responses to such stimuli are 'truly' different depending on whether we are alone or with others. Do we have a stronger desire to communicate our feelings if others are present? Do we try harder to share or hide our reactions? Is it different when playing in a drama, a romcom or a sitcom?

Variation: dealing with your baggage. The above exercise can be adapted to dealing with carrying weight, especially luggage. The laws of gravity and friction are not within the control of the actor and it is recommended that if a suitcase is supposed to be crammed full of clothes or dollar bills, then the props should be filled appropriately. (Paper can be substituted for cash!). Only then will the bags hang from the hand correctly or travel through the air believably as they are loaded onto the luggage rack. Even the sound of an empty bag is different. It can be fun to try to 'act' an empty bag as heavy but few will manage to convey this convincingly.

You don't have to watch much screen drama to observe actors having problems with luggage and, above all, with drinks, especially hot drinks. Only in screen drama can black coffee come straight from the vending machine and be slurped back with such relish. Only in TV drama can disposable cups, supposedly full of hot drinks, be swigged back or waved around with such abandon and set down on desks with that give-away hollow 'clack'. In TV drama the teacups are never full (and rarely contain hot or even brown liquid) and endless pints of beer are bought and left standing on the bar as the plot whistles on.

All the exercises cited so far involve improvisation, a most valuable tool in practising the experience of it never having happened before – because, by definition, it hasn't. Improvisation also involves the actors in listening and responding, and working with others in a truly ensemble manner (see Chapter 7). Holding on to the discoveries made during an improvisation can be a real challenge, and actors must practise reproducing these truths as if for the first time in subsequent performances. This is what they will have to do as different angles and takes are recorded.

EXERCISE 5:4 'THIS IS MY FIRST TIME' DUOS

Further exercises on those skills can be found in other chapters, but here we include one short exercise that tests many of the ideas in this chapter. The actors work in pairs and are given a two-line dialogue. The camera can be fixed on the actors (probably an upper-body two-shot is best). The actors are either already in position or move onto their marks. To look natural on screen they may have to stand 'unnaturally' close to each other. (See Chapter 9). The dialogue is started by A and responded to by B, followed by a pause, and then started by B, completed, followed by a pause, started by A and so on. It may help if after each round the actors step away, turn and step back onto their marks. This gives a moment's headspace to tackle the next version of the dialogue. Alternatively, the group of students can be paired off and the camera panned round from pair to pair, who in turn present a version of the dialogue:

A. I've got some news
B. What is it?
(pause)
B. I've got some news
A. What is it?
(pause)
A. I've got some news
B. What is it?
(pause)

... and so on. The actors are free to leave a pause, if appropriate, before the 'what is it?' line.

In each case the initiator of the dialogue has decisions to make. Who am I? What is my relationship with this person? What sort of news do I bear? Do I want to share it? Do I have to share it? Do I expect it to be well received? Do I expect an argument to follow? Do I feel guilt? Pride? Surprise?

The responder in the dialogue will also have to make decisions, whilst reacting to the tone and body language of her fellow actor. She may respond to his excited tone with delighted anticipation. But equally, she may respond with suspicion. If the initial line is presented with a sense of foreboding or guilt, the response may be one of empathetic support, fear or nonchalance. This exercise helps training screen actors understand that the script they are given contains endless possibilities and the way lines are played is a decision they have to make in light of their understanding of the character, their relationships with other characters and the demands of the director.

In this exercise the actors don't know what the subtext of the line they are receiving will be until they hear it. They have to listen and work out immediately the relationship and the import of the words from their own perspective.

Screen performances to consider

It is difficult to give examples of performances where remembering not to anticipate can be seen since we do not notice when things are going right. Performances in which anticipating or 'telegraphing' are evident tend to be quickly forgotten outside of 'blooper' compilations. Consider for example, though, the 'Here's Johnny' scene from *The Shining* (Stanley Kubrick, 1980). Bearing in mind that the scene is made up of several shots, Wendy (Shelley Duvall) has to maintain her terrified reaction throughout the different takes. Each time she 'does not know' what is going to happen. Similarly, when Jack Nicholson finally breaks through the door with the axe and reaches for the key, he gives us a genuinely convincing reaction to being slashed by Wendy's knife. This scene would not work, and would be far less terrifying, if there was even a hint that the actors had read the script. But they had – even though Nicholson's last line of the scene ('Here's Johnny') was improvised.[5]

[5]Martha Cliff, 'The Iconic Movie Scenes You Never Knew Were IMPROVISED', MailOnline, 2 May 2017. Available at: https://www.dailymail.co.uk/femail/article-4465202/The-iconic-movie-scenes-never-knew-IMPROVISED.html [accessed 20 May 2019]. The scene can be viewed at: https://www.youtube.com/watch?v=d-ABIIZV3vA [accessed 25 July 2018].

A comic example of genuinely working from moment to moment without anticipation is Steve Huison's reaction in *The Full Monty* (Peter Cattaneo, 1997). When his fellow brass bandsmen unexpectedly break into a rendition of *The Stripper*, his first reaction is confusion as he checks his music and wonders what he's got wrong. Then comes realization, followed by a range of beautifully modulated reactions ending with him accepting and even enjoying the joke being played at his expense.

More questionable is the performance of William Shatner in *Star Trek II: The Wrath of Khan* (Nicholas Meyer, 1982). In the scene where Kirk finds out for the first time that the *Enterprise* is under attack from his nemesis Khan, it could be argued that he (and the rest of the cast, perhaps) is anticipating this. The script then demands that Kirk tricks Khan into dropping his ship's protective shields in order to receive a transmission of the Genesis project data. At this moment the *Enterprise*'s counter-attack will begin. It is said that William Shatner insisted on delivering the line that signals this attack ('Here it comes – now') in his usual stylized-ironic staccato tone, and it took Meyer multiple shots to wear him down until he was so tired that he delivered the line in the required undertone. Meyer presumably felt that Shatner's standard style of delivery was too knowing and would, logically, alert Khan to the danger.[6]

Sometimes it is genuinely surprising that an error of anticipation has slipped through the editing process and passed the director: especially when the director is Alfred Hitchcock. In *North by Northwest* (1959) a young actor centrally seated in the background of the scene clearly anticipates the firing of a gun. Whilst the rest of the diners are engaged in merry conversation, the young actor covers his ears, knowing that a shot is about to be fired.[7]

A good example of working in the moment (and a personal favourite) occurs in the final scene of *Billy Elliot* (Stephen Daldry, 2000) where Billy's father, carrying with him all the emotional and financial struggle that has led to this point, sees the powerful mature ballerino take to the stage in the lead role in *Swan Lake*. The reaction, from Gary Lewis, consisting

[6]'Star Trek II Wrath of Khan– Reliant vs Enterprise; First Clash', YouTube.com, uploaded by Prometheus of Videos, 11 April 2015. Available at: https://www.bing.com/videos/search?q=Star+Trek+II+the+wrath+of+Kham+Attack+begins&view=detail&mid=E337C8EDAD37A22262FCE337C8EDAD37A22262FC&FORM=VIRE [accessed 25 July 2018].

[7]'North by Northwest Funny Goof', YouTube.com, uploaded by mikissi, 5 November 2008. Available at: https://www.youtube.com/watch?v=sAhKLfzDHcI [accessed 25 July 2018].

'merely' of an intake of breath, carries a wealth of emotion and pride. In that one second he shows that it was all worth it.[8]

Screen Actors' Motto #5:
Don't answer the phone until it rings.

[8]'Billy Elliott – The Final Scene', YouTube.com, uploaded by Tim R, 7 April 2013. Available at: https://www.bing.com/videos/search?q=Billy+Elliot+Ending+Scene&&view=detail&mid=B2E3E58798FF2A9B71D2B2E3E58798FF2A9B71D2&&FORM=VRDGAR [accessed 16 May 2018].

6 WHERE AM I? *WHEN* AM I?

To the actor

It's a real challenge, this acting stuff. You got yourself an agent, who got you an audition, and then you got the part by giving the casting director or director what they thought they needed. You got the script, did your homework, put on the costume and now, here you are, surrounded by people you don't know doing things you don't understand, using a barely recognizable language as they adjust lenses and sound equipment and shine lights in your face, flap about with sheets of reflective and coloured gel, and dance professionally around the omnipresent tripping hazards. Eventually, some sort of calm descends and the director or AD asks the actors to take their starting positions. Whilst the cacophony of technical preparation reduces to a burble, you may get some last-minute instructions about the scene and the take, when to move, where to arrive, things to avoid and things to ensure happen correctly. The burble descends further to become whispered comments. The hairstylist dashes forward to sweep back your hair that has flopped over your eyes. Wardrobe adjusts your collar. Continuity turns the bottle on the table, adjusting it by perhaps two millimetres to hide the logo. And you? You feel as though you are the centre of all this attention, even though everyone is actually getting on with their own jobs. You are trying to recall your lines and all the instructions and notes, whilst at the same time trying to build belief amongst all this twenty-first-century technical chaos that you are sitting in the court of the king, whom who you will advise, as courtier or queen perhaps, on matters of state. You have got to accept, and thus make us accept, that this is a palace in 1624. Yes, it's tough this acting malarkey.

> The camera … is not a recording device, it's a microscope which reveals what the eye does not see. It also penetrates into a person, under the surface display, and records thoughts and feelings – whatever is going on. (Kazan 1988: 187)

Research

Let's go back over how you prepared for this moment. Even for the audition, you will have acquainted yourself with as much detail about the project as you were able to glean. If you knew a little about the film's setting, your backstory prep will have involved historical research into such matters as the physical and vocal life of aristocrats of the time (as far as this is possible), including the pronunciation of unfamiliar words. You will have considered the nature of their backgrounds, how they would have interacted with those of higher and lower status. If you are the king's queen or advisor, there are decisions to be made. But, calm down. You *can* do this because you got the part.

Vocal life is about how the character speaks, taking account of class, background, education, regional accent, health, age and the given circumstances (e.g. am I trying to impress/fit in?). It will be related to your research into your backstory.

Yes, you got the part, and the contract and script duly landed in your mailbox. You create your backstory that, on this occasion, may also include:

- Information about the character from specific (was s/he a real person?) or general research.
- Do you (or the director) want the character to remain ambiguously motivated until the dénouement?

Let's consider this for a moment. In our example it may be that the counsel you are giving the king is unknowingly (one interpretation) or knowingly (a second interpretation) bad advice. This will probably be clear from the screenplay as a whole. But is your character wilfully misleading the king, or not?

Motivations

This is where you need to decide what your motivations are: why does the character do what they do? Is your motive one of self-interest, perhaps hoping to topple the king and rule in his place? Are you secretly in the pay of a foreign government? How easy is it for your character to mask his or her falsehood? All these questions will affect how to deal with the subtext of the script that arrives with the contract! Even when you have sorted all this out in your head, further options remain. Do you play the scene so that it is obvious to the viewer that you are being duplicitous? Or do you play the character's honesty unreservedly, allowing the treachery to be unmasked only later in the narrative? In procedural dramas, especially police/suspect interview scenes, this is a very common dilemma. Give the director something: don't try to be neutral. Give an interpretation that follows your instincts as an actor in this place, in this film, on this shoot, working with this director. If the director wants an adjustment, she will let you know. And because you have read Chapter 3 on 'the actor as plumber', you will be ready to oblige.

> Acting is behaving truthfully under imaginary circumstances. (Sanford Meisner, quoted in Silverberg 1994: 9)

So, you are ready to go, with all this information buzzing in your head and competing for attention. Now you have to enter the world of the film. When the director calls 'Action!', all the paraphernalia of the shoot, all the teams of people carrying out their roles, all disappear. There is just you, the other characters, the set and props: the world of the film. You are in a twilight existence where your acting takes over, whilst at the same time a distant part of your own brain keeps a watchful eye on what you are doing, reminding you about moves you must make, tones you must take, motives that you have and objectives you must chase. This small part of your brain is also on the alert for the call to 'Cut!' It is the only thing you are programmed to hear from outside the world of the shoot. And whether the scene reached its end or has been halted for another reason, you the actor step forward, displacing your character, and await further instructions, paying close attention to any changes required. Then it's back to the twilight zone for 'Action!'

To get to this point the research you have undertaken will be of central importance. Maybe you have had to learn how to use a quill (how many words can you write before you have to dip the pen into the inkpot again?). Perhaps you have to know how to use sealing wax and a signet ring. Having this tactile relationship with these objects will, like the costume you wear and the lines you say, feed your imagination and help transport you into the world of the film. If you can't accept that the powder you sprinkle on the document will dry the ink, then we won't be convinced that you know what you are doing. Such actions would be second nature to this courtier or queen.

We have mentioned the advisability of reading about the historical period to help you flesh out and create a backstory for your character. This would be as true for a shoot set in the 1930s depression, or in the Second World War or an inner-city gangland, as it is for our seventeenth-century example. Additionally, we would advise researching visual material: paintings and, for projects set during the last hundred years or so, photographs and documentaries. Even other films set in a similar period might be useful, though you always risk compounding and continuing the errors of others and being influenced by other actors' interpretations. When you get to the film set, whether you are surrounded by a genuine historic location or a castle made of polystyrene, you will have in your mind this wealth of knowledge about where and when you are. Where am I? When am I? It is your job to convince us that you inhabit this world and always have.

> When my partner is playing a king, I treat him like a king, and behave towards him as a person and not as the character of a king. Otherwise I will be using clichés. I must continuously adapt to a mind on the move. (Stanislavski, quoted in Benedetti 2005: 135)

In Stanislavskian terms, of course, this relates to defining your previous and given circumstances. If you look as if you have just beamed down onto the set, it will show. When you enter through those huge oak doors studded with iron (and actually made of plywood with lumps of black plastic – they'll add the creaking in post-production), as well as knowing your objective (why you are entering the room), you will know where you have come from, how far, what the weather was like and whether you have just got off a horse. Once in the room, you will only notice the things that belong to this world. The cables on the floor, the monitor glowing in the corner and even the safety pin holding your fellow actor's ruff together will remain unnoticed (though you still won't trip over the cables). Comey calls this the Art of Acceptance and defines it thus:

> Acceptance of the imaginary situation *as if* it were real allows you to be emotionally effective. Acting on film is not reality but a composite of imaginary circumstances and relationships. (Comey 2002: 117; emphasis in original)

He goes on:

> [You need to] put yourself mentally in that circumstance, suspend your judgment and disregard anything that is contradictory to the realness of the situation ... [Y]our ability to accept imaginary circumstances determines the truth of your performance. (Ibid.)

Totally immersing yourself in who, where and when you are links closely to the material covered in Chapter 7: Are you listening to me? How would your character respond to the 'offers' made and the situations that arise in the scene? In accepting the where and when of the scene, how will your character's objectives be met or thwarted by what happens?

Offer. An improv term meaning an action or piece of dialogue that opens the way for the response from others. In scripted material such as a film, it can include the way the line is delivered (see 'subtext'), which opens up possibilities. Even an aggressive, stonewalling delivery of a line can be an offer as it may give the responder a useful key to unlocking the delivery of their next line.

This is another area in which the skills and techniques of the screen actor differ from those of the theatre actor. In a theatre production you will be working within an environment created by the set, the lights and sound. Distinct demands will be made on the audience to 'suspend their disbelief' and accept that they can look through this fourth wall to watch the action, and that, for the most part, actors place themselves where they can be seen through this invisible wall. The audience will be buying in to the fallacy that the action of the play is happening and using their own imaginations to a high degree to create the truth of this fictive world in which they lose themselves.

> Like any artist, the actor has to be open to inspiration, intuition, and the unconscious. When you know what you are looking for, that's all you get. But when you're open to what's possible, you get something new. And that's creativity. (Alan Alda, quoted in Comey 2002: 167)

We would argue that film and television drama (as currently envisaged and realized) asks far less of the audience. Every effort will have been made to make the locations and settings as accurate as possible (even fantasy films will have their own coherence and believability). Costume and props will have been researched in minuscule detail. The blood and autopsies will look real – even in HD close-up. If a car from the wrong historical period appears on the road, or an anachronistic style of window is visible in the shot, there will be letters and tweets. It all has to be so real. The audience will not accept the 'where and when' of the film if these details are incorrect. And that goes for the acting too. You have to be totally immersed in this world, whether it is the royal court or the forensics lab. You need to belong there in order for us to believe you belong there and that the 'there' is real.

We can perhaps learn something from children in this respect. The reason that we often see such strong performances from children on screen is not that they have had years of studying Stanislavski and Adler and Strasberg and Meisner, but that they have not lost that ability to lose themselves in the world of their imagination. In the moment they can slip into the part, and slip out of it just as smoothly when it's time for lunch. Our acting technique should be emulating this skill. Often, as characters, we have to say and do the meanest things to people who may, in our real lives, be close friends whom we respect. But there is no room for pretence or 'demonstrating' these actions and words. We have to find something within ourselves to motivate them. This can be a real challenge if we haven't found that portal into the fictional world around us. Perhaps this is why actors have a reputation for hugging each other; when you come back through this portal, all you want to do is say, 'I'm so sorry! I didn't mean it: I was only acting!'

"When I was doing extra work at Shepperton Studios in the early 2000s, I was asked if I wanted to be a 'special extra'. That simply meant I would get paid extra if I didn't mind kissing a girl in a scene on set. I was up for that and so I went to the studios for the day's shoot. That day fifty extras were going to be used in a 1920s ballroom scene. The third AD came up to the group and she called my name out. I walked over to her. Then, speaking in a loud voice to all the other extras, she said, 'Who doesn't mind kissing Richard in a scene?' Silence. No one spoke out and no one moved. It felt like for ever. It was very embarrassing, and humiliating too! 'I know there are a lot of you who put your names down as special extras, who have signed up for kissing and I don't want to have to call you all out. So who is going to kiss Richard in the next scene?' Silence once more, nothing. 'Alright!' she said, and proceeded to call three girls out. I had to kiss a girl in the background of the ballroom scene, halfway up a flight of stairs. The first girl they chose kept telling me that it didn't mean anything and that she had a boyfriend. She kept on avoiding kissing me and they had to cut and get the next girl in. The second girl again tried to avoid kissing me and so she was removed as well. The director was getting very angry at this stage. The third girl was very friendly. She was well up for kissing me, thank God! The director told me to kiss the girl first standing up on the steps and then to lower her down while still kissing, so we were finally lying on the steps. This was rather tricky as she had a big dress on and we had to do it slowly. I was so focused on both making sure I was kissing her properly and lowering her down safely on the steps that every time they said 'Cut!' we both didn't hear it. They had to keeping saying 'Cut!' several times until we stopped – slightly embarrassing after all that had gone before.

A lot of fuss, embarrassment and humiliation could have been avoided if the third AD didn't make it public that they wanted a volunteer to kiss me. If she asked in private on a one-to-one basis without me being there, it all would have worked out fine. I enjoyed working with that actress but I never saw her again, which is a pity as, at the very least, I wanted to know why she didn't mind kissing me. – Richard Knight, actor

Some directors, to help actors find this acceptance of time and place, and perhaps not sufficiently trusting of the art of the actor to achieve this on their own, place them in quasi-real situations without rehearsal. Some examples of this are given at the end of this chapter. But you should first rely on your character and contextual research, backstory, identification of given and previous circumstances and your objectives to allow your character to know exactly where and when they are.

To the tutor

There are two main elements to the skills outlined in this chapter. The first is for the actor to take on fully the relationship with the other characters within the logic of the scene or screenplay, and the second is to totally acknowledge the temporal circumstances of the scene. A scene will play very differently depending where and when it is taking place. The exercises that follow are designed to allow the actors to creatively hone these skills. To do so successfully they will have to decide *who* they are (backstory, previous circumstances) before they can enter the world of these exercises, at which point they will need to know where and when they are.

EXERCISE 6:1 I WAS JUST SITTING THERE ...

This exercise can be undertaken by single actors or large groups. It will be necessary to decide where they are – spooky house, walking on the street, in the forest, in class, at home, in bed. Select something appropriate for the size of the group. Their job is to build belief in their activity (what are their objectives?), which is then interrupted by an unexpected sound that will change their objectives and cause them to react. You could have these sounds on tape or mark them with a visual or vocal signal. Possibilities include a creaking floorboard, a striking clock, music, gunshots, tyres squealing, 'is someone calling me?' and so on.

Variation. If you want to play around with the intensity of the reaction the sound incites, you could repeat the exercise several times indicating a number on a scale of 1–5 for the size of reaction required, thus introducing a modicum of direction into the scene. Alternatively, suggest a genre for the response in order to explore notions of comic and dramatic reaction.

In re-viewing the scene, students should discuss the probable location and backstory of the actor/s involved and consider how well a 'where' and 'when' was conveyed, as well as the truthfulness of the reaction.

EXERCISE 6:2 SCARY AND SHOUTY

Our first reaction to the script or screenplay can be to plunge for the obvious without really considering the 'where' and 'when' of the action. This can lead to demonstrated performances based in stereotypes. In performance, and in audition, such obvious portrayals should be avoided. Once again the actors should have a strong notion of their backstory and relationship before undertaking the exercise. The objective of B is clear (or is it?) and A must be sure she know what she is doing before B's line cuts across and changes her reaction.

Allow the actors to follow their instincts in the following scene:

Character A is waiting to order a drink at a bar.
Suddenly, off camera, a loud angry voice can be heard shouting:
B. [OOV] I'm going to kill you!
(The camera stays on A's face in close-up. B comes over to A and the camera picks up the two-shot. Cut.)

This scene is re-viewed and the actors' success in creating the 'when' and 'where' of the piece is analysed. This may produce different interpretations, such as:

- a bar in a Western
- a bar in 1930s Chicago
- a bar in a London pub as part of a soap opera
- an exclusive wine bar
- a bar in a sci-fi movie
- a bar in a comedy Western.

The playing of this scene might be very different for each of these. Also, are there other people around? Are either of the characters drunk? Discussions will throw up many possibilities for this 'simple' two-line scene and different pairs can demonstrate their ability to 'accept' successfully the version they undertake. For example, the exercise could be repeated with character A waiting to order the drink at the bar as character B (unseen at the beginning of the previous shoot) now quietly walks to the bar and stands besides A (Figure 10). B pauses for a moment, then whispers very gently into A's ear: 'I'm going to kill you!'

FIGURE 10 Exercise 6:2 Scary and Shouty. Photo by Abby Timms.

As well as identifying the belief in the 'when' and 'where' of the scene, viewers could also consider issues of script interpretation. Which of A's reactions portrays more fear? Shoot 1 or Shoot 2? If it were a real situation, which would you find more frightening and why?

How else could you play the scene? What might you try in an audition? Post-discussion, the scene is reset and shot with two different students and the process repeated, always seeking a truthful recognition of the time and place.

EXERCISE 6:3 THE CORPSE AT THE FUNERAL

I was once at a wedding where the bridegroom was totally overtaken by a fit of the giggles. The more he tried to control them the worse they got and the more distressed his bride and the families became. He was helpless with laughter and could do nothing but try to blurt out his vows whilst tears of laughter flowed down his face. This exercise allows the actors to enjoy such a moment. The situation is given: it's a funeral. The actors or tutor can determine the historical period, which will affect the formality of the proceedings. The actors need to know their relationship and attitude to the deceased.

Characters A and B are standing at the graveside, or sitting in the church or chapel, shoulder to shoulder. Off camera, a third actor delivers the eulogy (the dialogue can be improvised or read from a pre-written text).

The whole scene is to be recorded in a medium two-shot. A, perhaps triggered by something in the eulogy, begins to corpse and struggles to stifle the laughter. The second character, B, clearly indignant at this social insensitivity, displays displeasure by nudging A, but only succeeds in making the giggling worse. In turn, character B begins to giggle and attempts to stifle it, whilst character A now has the giggles under control and reverses the action by nudging character B. Both actors now regain their composure, momentarily. Eventually, both actors burst into laughter. Cut.

In the re-viewing, the group should discuss the truthfulness of the performance given the situation. Was the physicality of stifled laughter natural or was it over the top? See if anyone in the group has memories of a similar situation they can share. It doesn't have to be a funeral, just any social situation where giggling or outright laughter was inappropriate.

Was the situation comic? Embarrassing? Where was the comedy in the scene? Was it because of the location? The acting? Could the scene be played without comedy?

The scene, post-discussion, is reset and shot with two different students on camera and one off camera and the whole process repeated.

Variation. You could involve the whole group in this exercise, experimenting with a 'Mexican wave' of giggling or individual outbreaks that are brought under control and then released again (Figure 11). The same issues of place and time are present as are questions of drama and comedy.

FIGURE 11 Exercise 6:3 The corpse at the funeral. Photo by Luigi Caramella.

EXERCISE 6:4 GOOD NEWS/BAD NEWS

In this scene (which needs to be learned or sight-read with confidence) one actor (A) is bringing news to B and C about a hospital visit. How the news is shared and how the emotional undercurrents are dealt with will depend on the location ('where') as well as the 'when' (what emotional state are each of them in?). Consideration needs to be given to the relationships and the backstory, which in turn will feed the objectives that each brings with them. For example, what does A want to achieve in this scene? What is B desperate to avoid? What is behind the enigmatic quietness of C?

The news may be good, bad or mixed. The actors should concentrate on responding to the reactions and needs of the other as they pursue their objectives, demonstrating appropriate acknowledgement of their location. Different trios can approach the piece in different ways within the parameters of the agreed time and place. For example:

- Playing the scene whilst carrying out a domestic activity – washing up, preparing food, ironing.
- Playing in the park with other people around, including children.
- Eating in a restaurant.
- In a library.
- At home in the evening reading the paper or using a mobile phone.
- In a bar.
- In the living room, with the children asleep upstairs.
- Or actually at the hospital, with the bustle of nurses and doctors around.

News from the hospital

A. (entering) Hi.

B. How is she?

A. Yeah.

B. Yeah?

A. Er, they didn't say a lot.
B. What did they say?
A. You know, tests and things.
B. Yeah?
A. Yeah.
B. Did they say how long she'll be there?
A. Why does that matter?
B. What?
A. I know it's difficult to have her with us.
B. I didn't say that. I've never said that.
C. Hmm.
B. You keep out of this.
A. Out of what? What's s/he been saying?
C. I'm keeping out of this.
B. I just asked how she's getting on.
A. She's not, really.
C. What?
B. (looks confused)
A. It's worse than they thought.
B. Oh, I … I … I'm so sorry. What did they say?
A. You won't have to worry about her coming back. (goes)
B. I didn't … I only meant … Shit!

Screen performances to consider

Some directors like to ensure that the reaction of their actors is totally real and try to thoroughly immerse them in the reality of the scene.

Perhaps one of the cruellest examples of a director plunging an actor into the reality of the film involved the actress Tippi Hedren. In order to capture a moment of genuine terror in *The Birds* (1963), the film's director, Alfred Hitchcock, allowed the use of real birds in one of the avian attack scenes instead of the mechanical ones Hedren had been promised.

She recalled:

> When I got to the set I found out there had never been any intention to use mechanical birds because a cage had been built around the door where I was supposed to come in, and there were boxes of ravens, gulls and pigeons that bird trainers wearing gauntlets up to their shoulders hurled at me, one after the other, for a week.[1]

In the film the look of sheer terror in Hedren's eyes is real. It is a tribute to her professionalism that she dealt with the unpredicted and viciously random pecking by not breaking the reality of the scene. Few professional directors would today go to such lengths when the wonders of CGI are at their disposal, but you might want to read the small print in your contract very carefully!

In an interview, actors in the drama series *Mad Men* (AMC, 2007–15) describe an infamous episode involving a sequence with a guy, a girl and a lawnmower. As dictated by the storyline, an incident occurs which affects onlookers, whose facial reactions are completely real. They were told, in rehearsal, that they would be sprayed with blood on a count of 'three' but the director and crew unleashed the bloody spray on 'two'. They were genuinely surprised and a little shaken.[2]

The first incarnation of Willy Wonka (*Willy Wonka and the Chocolate Factory*, Mel Stuart, 1971) starred Gene Wilder as the offbeat Wonka. Stuart ensured that none of the actors in the scene knew about the set of the chocolate room and candy gardens, so that when they enter the room, it's the actors who are seeing it for the first time, and their looks of amazement and wonder are genuine.[3]

In *Alien* (1979), Ridley Scott kept from the actors the horror of the scene in which the alien bursts from John Hurt's stomach.[4] They'd

---

[1]John Hiscock, *Daily Telegraph*, 24 December 2012.

[2]See: https://uproxx.com/tv/mad-men-lawnmower-scene-oral-history [accessed 12 July 2018].

[3]'Trivia', IMDb.com. Available at: https://m.imdb.com/title/tt0067992/trivia [accessed 14 June 2018]. 'Pure Imagination – Gene Wilder – Willy Wonka', YouTube.com, uploaded by MoviesMusicNature, 31 October 2011. Available at: https://www.bing.com/videos/search?q=candy+gradens+willy+wonka+gene+wilder&view=detail&mid=5D0CD390FA864D7A08855D0CD390FA864D7A0885&FORM=VIRE [accessed 14 June 2018].

[4]'Chestburster Scene from Alien (1979)', YouTube.com, uploaded by Adriaan Odendaal, 29 July 2013. Available at: https://www.youtube.com/watch?v=LsD6AL3HJtM [accessed 20 May 2019].

discussed it in theory, but for the shoot Scott had four cameras running and allowed the horror of the moment to hit the actors for the first time, without rehearsal. Sigourney Weaver remarks:

> Look, I worked with Roman Polanski on *Death and the Maiden* – he would shoot a gun off. You can act, sure, but when you're surprised, that's gold.[5]

According to Comey, Jack Nicholson maintained that 'in acting, it's best if you really don't know' (Comey 2002: 68). You may or may not agree!

Finally, there is the renowned scene from *Midnight Cowboy* (John Schlesinger, 1968). According to Dustin Hoffman, the altercation with the taxi driver was real and his lines to cover it were improvised. However, it is more likely that the decision was made to include this real encounter in the film and the famous 'I'm walkin' here!' scene was reshot, with a supporting artist driving the taxi.[6] Perhaps what the scene really shows is the benefits that come from immersing yourself in the character and situation; knowing where and when you are.

Screen Actors' Motto #6:
Enter the where, believe the when.

---

[5] 'The Making of Alien's Chestburster Scene', interview with the cast and crew, *The Guardian*, 13 October 2009. Available at: https://www.theguardian.com/film/2009/oct/13/making-of-alien-chestburster [accessed 25 July 2018].

[6] Brian Cronin, 'Movie Legends: The Truth Behind the Famous "I'm Walkin' Here" Scene', CBR.com, 15 October 2017. Available at: https://www.cbr.com/midnight-cowbody-im-walkin-here/ [accessed 11 May 2019].

7 ARE YOU LISTENING TO ME?

All one wants to see from an actor is the intensity and accuracy of their listening.

ALAN RICKMAN[1]

To the actor

'Breakfast is ready!' Information affects us. What happens when somebody shouts this invitation to you? Maybe a visualization of bacon, eggs, sausages, beans, toast (two slices, buttered), mushrooms and a mug of coffee. Healthier breakfasts are available but this one sounds really nice. Your second thought may be to get to the feast as quickly as possible. The verbal message kickstarts a physical and sensory response and if the breakfast is cooked for you as a special treat, it could ignite an emotional reaction. But if somebody shouts, 'The taxman's at the door!', your response would probably be to run for the hills. (Naturally, we are not condoning this course of action.)

Communication

Effective communication requires a sender and a receiver. Somebody 'says' and Somebody 'listens'. When 'A' says something to 'B', then usually the information contained is something 'A' has thought about.

[1]'Alan Rickman on Importance of Listening When Acting', interview with Tim Sebastian, *HardTalk* (2010), YouTube.com, published by BBC News, 14 January 2016. Available at: https://www.youtube.com/watch?v=BfytKK6gyVE [accessed 13 October 2018].

Unless of course it is an argument where unthinking verbal missiles are delivered rapidly without any consideration to feelings or surroundings.

How many shouty, real-life public arguments have *you* witnessed? If none, you are lucky but you probably need to get out more. If you have stumbled across one, ask yourself – did the arguers seem aware of people passing when in the heat of the confrontational furnace? Was the delivery of the angry words clear, precise, well thought out and logical, or were they erratic and ungrammatical? Were they *really* listening to each other? Or just responding by shouting at and over each other? Did they walk away hand in hand after a resolution or part separately, storming off in different directions, leaving the scene of the whine not having heard a word during the verbal altercation and vowing mentally to call Jerry Springer?

In real life, such confrontational moments are usually both clumsy and unintelligible. This is not to say that film arguments cannot be loud, disruptive and seemingly out of control. The very fact that they *are* in control is what makes them understandable. One of the great examples of this is the explosive and dramatic *Who's Afraid of Virginia Woolf?* (Mike Nichols, 1966). Elizabeth Taylor and Richard Burton portray an embattled and bitter married couple whose personal barbs are full of raging torment. Every vicious insult drips with animosity, venom and contempt. Every spat word is designed to create gaping emotional wounds. Words become weapons. The screenplay provides the verbal bullets and the characters fire the ammunition on the battlefield of their lives.

Read the original play by Edward Albee and imagine how the conversations might sound. Then watch the film. Are the two main actors, Taylor and Burton, listening to each other? Really listening? Yes, but are the *characters* listening to each other? How will you know the difference? Listen to the rhythm; it never lies. In film, the intentions and delivery have to be clear or the viewer will become embroiled in a storytelling mess that demands a refund from the box office. See (or maybe not) *The Room* (Tommy Wiseau, 2003). Listen to the rhythm in this one if you can find it. Consider yourself warned!

Not all communication has to be loud and confrontational. The softly spoken and heartfelt 'I love you, will you marry me?' is sure to get a response. (It may not be the response you want, so do keep the receipt for the ring safe.) Usually:

- A message sent contains information that will ignite the response – even if that response is given through silence. It is an 'offer'.

- A response will be dictated by the receiver's understanding – or misunderstanding – of the information.
- A verbal message cannot be effective dramatically if the receiver is not listening.

Often the message isn't clear. What if the sender talks in a manner that requires the receiver to decipher what the real meaning is? The best of dramatic writing engages with its intriguing possibilities. Sometimes two people (or more) skirt around the real issue by delivering conversation in a deliberately coded form using subtext; hiding a secret, for example, or fearful of the possible response once the information is divulged. Many of the exercises outlined in this book thus far can be explored in this way.

Sometimes the novice actor can get caught up in the delivery of their dialogue and forget other important aspects of performance. If your contribution to the shooting of a scene with another actor is to solely wait for your 'bit' to say, then problems will arise when the footage eventually reaches the editor. If you weren't listening truthfully, then your responses, born of your inner monologue, will be absent.

- The editor's solution, through judicious cutting, may be to favour your fellow actor talking.
- With no clear 'listened to' reactions, there may be nothing of value in your performance to cut to.
- If there is nothing to cut to, then most of your performance may end up on the edit floor.
- By not listening in a film scene, you may just edge yourself out of the shot.
- By not listening in a film audition, you may just edge yourself out of a job (more about that in Chapter 11).

The actor/character as good listener

- To be a good listener is to go deeper than simply waiting for the other actor to finish what they are saying.
- Listening is to instantly respond to emotions *as they arise.*

- Listening is being able to accommodate subtleties that didn't present themselves in rehearsal.
- Listening informs the response of both the verbal and physical.

Listening facilitates an energetic and emotional flow from one actor to another.

> *"Give your all for your scene partner's close-up as well as your own – this will never go unappreciated and is only fair – acting is reacting after all! I've had to play an emotional scene to the side of someone's head who was not engaged at all and just stood there with their arms folded whilst I gave my all. – Sarah Leigh, actor*

The actor/character as bad listener

- A bad listener is one who is simply waiting for the other to give them the cue to speak.
- They respond not through emotion but through the lines as written, leaving out the nuances of subtext.
- The bad listener turns a natural response into an automated, even exaggerated, one.
- The bad listener misses 'offers'.
- The bad listener can cause the other actor to overact, forcing them to compensate for the lack of communication.

Try this: observe yourself listening in a situation when you really want to communicate. Be aware of your physicality and how this is affected by location, ambient noise and the substance of the dialogue. Perhaps you lean in towards the person you are listening to, or squint with concentration or look down, considering the impact of what you are hearing. You place your focus solely on them, you don't 'turn off', unless this is your deliberate response to what they are saying – but even that is communication, for you are communicating that you don't intend to listen.

Perhaps you may *want* to give your full attention to something else. This rejection might manifest itself with a sharp 'leave me alone' shrug of the shoulders and may even lead to one of those very public arguments we mentioned earlier. (Come to think of it, have you still got the engagement ring receipt handy?) Listening requires a response. It's the same with acting, which is why we emphasize listening so much in this book.

> *"I think one of the most crucial aspects of screen acting are your eyes – they really do give away your true feelings more on camera than in life. During one of my first films, I appeared in a dialogue scene with another actor. I was unaware that for the entire take both our faces were in shot and as a result when it was my turn to listen as the other guy spoke, I switched off thinking the camera couldn't see me. Twelve years on I still cringe when I see it – my eyes are lifeless and give the impression that I wasn't listening! The lesson is 'know your framing and never let your eyes go dead, not for even a second' – the camera and the audience will see it! – Robin Kirwan, actor*

As an actor, you nurture and protect your craft by delivering the best you can. Thinking, feeling, listening actors want to create strong and emotionally believable connections between the characters. That's the job. Don't ignore any of the skills required to complete that job or it may be your last. The costumier wouldn't be employed if they didn't know how to thread a needle, or imagine a sound operator not bothering to check the boom, a cameraperson not storing a roll of finished film, the director spending time on their mobile phone whilst you are trying to act. These situations all amount to exactly the same thing: somebody is not concentrating on their job. A thoughtless contribution to a work in progress is a weak link and everybody on a film set will underachieve.

Silence and listening

Verbally dramatic moments are usually contrasted with others of silence. As examples of this balance we recommend *Rififi* (Jules Dassin, 1955) and *Hostiles* (Scott Cooper, 2017). You may ask what has silence got to do with listening?

- In life we let others speak in whatever way they wish, unless we are directly threatened.
- We 'hear' emotions even when words are not spoken and need to be alert to the offered connection. Polar opposite examples could be the anger of a fist hitting a fridge or the relaxed lyrical whistling of somebody as they thumb through a catalogue.

The act of listening is an act of discovery. Consider the dinner sequence between Helen Keller and Annie Sullivan as portrayed respectively by Patty Duke and Anne Bancroft in *The Miracle Worker* (Arthur Penn, 1962). It is an almost silent scene within a talking film. The actors communicate through the physical rather than the verbal. They still listen to each other. They still hear each other.

If it is done correctly, a film will encourage the audience to contemplate every nuance of the dialogue as brought to life by the images presented. They will become emotionally invested with what is happening on the screen through engagement with characters as defined by plot, dialogue, body language, action, reaction. They will wait for the characters to communicate in order to fully realize and understand the story. None of this communication would be of any dramatic value without complete sensory engagement by the actors. Sharing is the key. When we speak in real life, we reveal something about ourselves even if we try desperately hard not to. In drama it is exactly the same – the sharing is done through the voice, the body and the facial expressions. It may seem obvious but if one person in a scene appears not to be listening to the other, then why should an audience listen? Why should they care if an actor doesn't?

Once you and your fellow actors engage with the giving and receiving of signs and signals (verbal and physical), you will quickly discover that you are working together in the same scene towards a desired or discovered effect. Remember, a director will not have time to teach you how and why you should listen to the character playing opposite you. That is something you bring to the set. The exercises in this chapter are designed to help you identify the power you can bring to your performance by being generous and receptive when working with others. And if you are playing a solo scene with no dialogue? Listening is still important, only this time the actor is listening to *the inner monologue* of the character.

A good example of this is the character Ivan Locke, as played by Tom Hardy in *Locke* (Steven Knight, 2013). Hardy's character spends the eighty-five minutes running time of the film responding to and dealing with mobile phone calls as he is driving. Other characters are only heard during the film via the mobile phone; they are not seen. Watch the actor engage the audience through his very visible listening skills. For the moments between the phone calls, the actor applies his actor's craft most convincingly as he silently digests each dilemma his character encounters. Whilst his body is physically hemmed in by the constraints of the car, the geography of his face is completely free.

Listening is not a passive activity, especially within performance relationships. In person, in a one-to-one conversation/altercation, we can physically see the other actor's body language. Equally, they can see ours. Over the phone we have to interpret, imagine and sense their physicality based on tone of delivery, and again vice versa. We have to listen. They have to listen. The challenge for you as a screen actor is to deal with listening whilst playing the scene as if you know nothing of what is happening or will happen. You may have rehearsed it a dozen times (or not at all) but once 'Action!' is called and that camera is turning, you and your fellow actor are saying the author's words for the first time.

You will have read the script and considered your character's backstory, motivations and objectives. You will be prepared to give a coherent portrayal of the character and to receive from your fellow actors their equally considered vision of their roles. However, you know what they are going to say (and maybe even do) and you will have formed some notion of *their* motivations and objectives.

It's not about you

It is at this point that you need to recognize that the scene is not about you.

- You need to hold on to your backstory and motivations but play only against what you *actually* receive on the set in the given moment.
- Realizing that the scene is not just about you will empower the act of listening.

- Listening is an act of generosity that undercuts any tendency to allow your egosystem to intervene.
- Resist the temptation to focus only on what your character wants to say.
- The emotions engendering the subtext of what is being said are more significant than the mere words.
- Stop thinking and concentrate on listening.

The director's role in these acts of giving and receiving is to negotiate with the actors which of the possibilities are going to serve the overall needs of the film. She or he may guide the actor to select a different aspect or emphasis of the subtext, which in turn will affect what is given and thus what is received. Some directors will rely more and others less on the instincts of the actors in this respect. But the actors need to understand that the choices they make and what they give on set will change what the other actors give back.

Listening will afford you the most power you will ever have in the process of the creation of the film. And that's well worth listening to.

To the tutor

Listening is sometimes taken for granted as distractions become normalized in our world. The ubiquitous mobile phone and its variety of ringtones cut through any other sound and seem designed to destroy the atmosphere of the acting workshop. Hard-earned and focused moments of character interaction can be destroyed by even one such interruption. The buzzing and ringing can suck the artistic air out of the action in progress very quickly. But rather than banning phones outright, it can be of great value to utilize them in the workshop.

EXERCISE 7:1 GETTING IN ON THE 'ACTION'

Here is a format that can be used in many of the exercises and which allows the use of mobile phone cameras to engage students in the processes of film. With larger groups it also facilitates more engagement with performance by a greater number.

- First set up the exercise to be shot and place the actors taking part in it.
- Instruct the rest of the students to switch off all notification sounds on their mobile phones.
- Split the cohort up into smaller groups.
- Each group is given a location in the room and a task.

The task is to use their phones in the following manner:

- Group 1: Is to shoot the exercises/action on the floor – in wide shot.
- Group 2: Is to shoot the exercises/action on the floor – in mid-shot.
- Group 3: Is to shoot the exercises/action on the floor – in close-up.
- Other groups can shoot the action from different angles, heights or distances.

Of course, the groups, just like everybody else involved, are to observe the rules of the process – i.e. 'Quiet on the set!' They film the action/exercises as they in turn are filmed by the main camera. The footage from the phones can be edited at a later stage to create a shooting diary or a workshop documentary (which students may prefer to keeping a logbook or journal). The 'crews' can still contribute to any discussions that take place after the exercise has been completed on the floor. The Q & A should also be filmed. This process can produce a unique record of that year's experience. And all of it without banning the phone.

EXERCISE 7:2 ARE YOU LISTENING? REALLY LISTENING?

- One actor tells an anecdote, real or imagined, whilst the other actor listens without responding vocally.
- The camera stays on the receiver's reaction/s.
- Play back and observe these reactions.
- Were they overplayed? Stereotyped? What were the feelings of each of the listeners? Of course, everything received has to be considered and reacted to.

EXERCISE 7:3 FEWER WORDS, MORE LISTENING

The inexperienced improviser – and equally, an egotistical improviser – will tend to fill the void of any exercise with words. That screen performances are rooted in words is a common misconception amongst enthusiastic young actors. The screen actor has to realize that film and most other screen dramas are visual media. (Invite students to watch any film whilst being aware of the balance of text and visual content.) The director and editor will decide what to use from the already pared-down script of the screenwriter and the various takes of the scene that the actor has provided. This exercise is designed to help screen actors become aware of the fact that, whilst the words may be few, the strength of their performance will lie in the communication that has taken place in the subtext underpinning those words, and especially the silences. We tell our students to 'trust the silence', for it is in this silence that the most powerful moments of ensemble performance can be found.

The actors are given a simple scenario to improvise. There is no need to record the initial improv. These can involve between two and five actors, though smaller numbers are more manageable. Here are some possible situations:

- A couple breaking up and deciding who owns what (two actors).
- A group of homeless people sitting under a bridge at night (up to five actors).
- Friends waking up after a sleepover following a party (up to five actors).
- Parents and child/ren at the breakfast table or in the car (three/four actors).
- Soldiers diffusing a bomb (two/three actors).
- Politicians during an election discussing strategy when things are going wrong (up to seven actors).

Allow the improvisation to run until a story/scenario has emerged. Ask the actors to choose just three of the things they said in the improvisation and then use these in a new distilled version. Take care that the camera operator shoots a mix of not only the deliverers of the lines but the reactions of those receiving them.

- This second improvisation has all the content of the first, but fewer of the words.
- There will be questions unanswered (why?), statements that are allowed to hang in the air, unspoken hints at feelings and relationships.
- Even if the actors use up all of their lines, the improvisation has a predetermined length (anything between two and five minutes).

If the actors have no lines left, they have to 'keep acting' until the director (you, the tutor) says 'Cut!' The actors have to make sense of the silences by sticking with the subtext and their knowledge of the situation. Replacement activities such as grunting or gesturing are discouraged unless justifiable from a character base!

We are looking here at the frisson created when actors imbue their lines with a subtext that governs how they give and how they respond not only to the words of others, but also to their body language and facial communication. This is also an exercise in concentration and requires the actor to be constantly aware of the other actors, remaining open to what is being given so that it impacts on what is given back in the scene. As film is a visual medium, often less is more.

What a script says that isn't dialogue is as important as the spoken word. I remember when Jane Fonda and I were doing the café scene in *Julia* [1977], the night before we shot, Fred Zinnemann said that he wanted us both to work on the scene to cut our own dialogue as much as possible – which we did. I thought, 'My God, this is brilliant.' … Some things will go, but on the other hand, if the director can communicate on film, things can be communicated that didn't need to be communicated in word. And, of course, we were not taking out each other's lines; we were taking out our own lines, anything that we considered superfluous.[2]

EXERCISE 7:4 MINI-DIALOGUES

This exercise is related to the previous one but gives the actors a short dialogue that can be memorized in a few seconds. The possible situations and subtexts underpinning the dialogues are endless, and this in itself is useful training for young actors, who might be tempted to go for the superficial meaning of the text rather than investigating whether their character, their backstory and the words given have a subtext. It is, after all, the subtext that should be guiding what they give the other actor and what they then will have to receive in return. It is helpful in this exercise to allow the actors to decide the basic parameters of the situation – who and where they are and the nature of the relationship (if any).

The camera can focus on a straightforward two-shot, but it may be more useful, if facilities allow, to intersperse this with close-ups not only of the speaker, but the listener; not only the giver, but the receiver.

Here are some sample dialogues:

#1

A. I know

B. You know

A. Tomorrow

B. I know

#2

A. It was there

B. Incredible concept really

A. Was it

B. Time flies

[2]Vanessa Redgrave, interview with Martin Sherman, *Interview* magazine, 12 January 2015. Available at: https://www.interviewmagazine.com/film/vanessa-redgrave.

#3

A. Desperate

B. The way it came across

A. How many colours

B. Baffling

#4

A. I don't understand

B. It's always like this

A. Meaningless

B. It's always like this

#5

A. Last time

B. Probably the same

A. I'm ready to go

B. Last time

#6

A. Fantastic

B. That's it

A. That's it

B. Please

#7

A. Hello

B. Hello

A. Been waiting long

B. Ages

Let us consider the first of these dialogues. It could be a discussion between two students about an exam:

A. (boastfully) I know

B. (dismissively) You know!

A. (taunting) Tomorrow!

B. (depressed) I know

If the delivery of the lines is given and received, then a clear relationship between the two characters will emerge. A is confident about the exam, B is not, A teases her and B gets depressed. Or:

A. (boastfully) I know
B. (you are irritating) You know!
A. (taunting) Tomorrow!
B. (Duh!) I know

The actors may decide that the discussion is between a child and an ageing parent on the eve of going into hospital. This was the situation selected by the actors in Figure 12:

A. (sighs, resigned) I know
B. (attempted cheerfulness) You know
A. (thoughtfully, under his breath) Tomorrow
B. (supportively) I know

FIGURE 12 Exercise 7:4 Mini-dialogues. Photo by Abby Timms.

Even with the same situation and characters, the lines can be given and received in a totally different way:

A. (I don't want to talk about it) I know!
B. (patronizing) You know
A. (I'm not stupid!) Tomorrow!
B. (I get that you're angry) I know!

All the dialogues can be experimented with in this way and will help screen actors approach a screenplay with an open mind: to look at not only the text, but the subtext. This subtext will then inform how they give their own performance and receive that of others as the overall interaction symbiotically emerges. Once again it can be useful in this exercise to introduce a time frame to encourage the use of pause and silence and to avoid the reliance on text alone to carry the scene forward.

EXERCISE 7:5 DID I HEAR YOU RIGHT?

This is a look at what we hear (!). The point of the exercise is for the group to try to figure out exactly what the characters are talking about. How important is the object? Has their relationship broken down? Are they lovers just joking with each other? The two actors should not make any decisions about the situation before they do it, though you may wish to draw their attention to the multiple possibilities contained in the text (Figure 13). They pick up each other's intention by the way they read into the delivery. It can be serious or light, sad, funny or vicious. The suspense is created by the journey from opening question to the final statement.

A. Did you see it?
(no response)
A. I asked you a question.
(response/action)
A. I'll ask you again.
B. I've seen it.
A. Where?
B. You're looking at it.
A. I'm … You're wearing it?
B. Do I look like I'm wearing it?
A. I …
B. I've eaten it.
A. You've …

B. Eaten it.
A. Why?
B. Because I knew you were looking for it.
A. Do you hate me that much?
B. Not that much ... more ... much, much more!

FIGURE 13 Exercise 7:5 Tutor setting up the scene for 'Did I hear you right?' Photo by Abby Timms.

Screen performances to consider

An example of chaotic control in an argumentative dialogue can be found in Robert Redford's film *Ordinary People* (1980). Three members of the same family sitting down to eat breakfast. Each of them wanting to be the best they can be in the eyes of the others – the best mother, the best father and the best son. These objectives descend into emotional chaos over the eating of French toast. In fact, eating the bread is a displacement activity for the real emotions they are having great difficulty discussing. The collective suffering, in the wake of tragic experiences, is heightened by the simplicity of sharing food – or attempting to. What makes the scene so powerful is that we, the viewer, can see and feel the intensity of the dialogue. View the scene. Watch how they listen to each other, and feel the bubbling, unspoken pain that lies beneath.

> I remind myself every morning: Nothing I say this day will teach me anything. So if I'm going to learn, I must do it by listening. (Larry King)[3]

The Oscar-winning actor Jeff Bridges discusses his very early screen experiences in relation to the edit in the documentary *Casting By* (Tom Donahue, 2012). In it there is a clip from *Halls of Anger* (Paul Bogart, 1970) that shows the young Bridges in a not too favourable acting light. In the documentary he explains how his acting technique at the time was emotionally way over the top, which is quite obvious to those who can bear to watch it. Bridges seems intent on focusing solely on the delivery of a highly charged performance. It is clear that he is *not listening* to the other actor in the scene, Calvin Lockhart. So much so that the editor of the film had to cut the scene around Bridges' energetic paroxysm. Luckily for Jeff Bridges, his acting career survived the professional embarrassment. His performances improved as he journeyed on to discover the value of the aural!

The actor Keanu Reeves is terrific in *John Wick* (Chad Stahelski and David Leitch, 2014), but one of his earlier screen performance deserves heavy criticism. He was cast as Jonathan Harker in director Francis Ford Coppola's version of *Dracula* (1992). The part required an upper-class English accent, which proved difficult for Reeves to master. He tried (too) hard and is visibly uncomfortable when he has something to say. Though clearly concentrating on delivering the lines, he seems not to be listening to the other actors. This is even more pointed in his scenes with Gary Oldman as Dracula. View the scenes and see what you think.

In *The Godfather* (referred to in Chapter 3), there is a sequence in a restaurant where Al Pacino's character Michael decides to murder two men who are at war with his father. They are rival gangster Sollozzo (Al Lettieri) and corrupt police captain McCluskey (Sterling Hayden). Pacino's acting task here is complex as he must convey to the audience his nervousness and doubt about the impending assassinations and the possible repercussions for his family. Watch Pacino 'listen' to the other characters as he goes through a moral crisis to arrive at his unavoidable action. He brilliantly captures the character's emotional state without

---

[3]'Larry King in Quotes', *The Telegraph*, 16 December 2010. Available at: www.telegraph.co.uk/culture/tvandradio/8207302/Larry-King-in-quotes.html [accessed 2 December 2018].

giving anything away to the other characters. Pacino is doing two things here: on the outside listening to the other two and on the inside listening to his conscience.

Consider also Meryl Streep's performance in *Sophie's Choice* (Alan J. Pakula, 1982) where her Meryl 'listening' skills are displayed in the most haunting fashion. An imprisoned Polish mother is forced to stand in line for a German concentration camp allocation with her young daughter and son. A Nazi officer demands that she choose which of her children will survive. One will live. One will die. It is an impossible and heartbreaking decision. Watch as Streep's character – Sophie – internalizes and tries to comprehend what has been suggested to her.

The turmoil leads to an astonishing 'silent scream' as Sophie's life-changing and life-ending choice is made.

Screen Actors' Motto #7:
If you're not listening, you're not acting.

8 WHERE WERE WE?

You must see if you can recreate this lost world.

STELLA ADLER, QUOTED IN KISSEL 2000: 113

To the actor

Have you ever woken up in a panic because you can't quite remember where you have to be that morning? Or what time you have to be there? Or who you have to see? Or what you might need to talk about? You leap out of bed and frantically search for that other sock as you try to insert a contact lens. And amidst the heart-pounding dash comes that persistent, nagging endless thought, 'Aargh, I wish I'd planned this better … yesterday!' Not a nice feeling. Now imagine a different day and you are standing in front of a large crowd of people. They are staring at *you*, waiting – waiting for something, anything. 'Action!' has just been called, but from you, the centre of attention in the scene about to be shot, comes nothing! No matter how much you scrunch your brow, crack your knuckles or wish for a sudden swirling tornado to appear and transport you way beyond the clouds to the Land of Oz, you just cannot remember what comes next. The last time you worked on this scene was three months ago! This is the pick-up shot! The one you knew was coming but quite possibly put to the back of your mind.

Remember, you are not alone in the fragmented shooting world; most actors have faced this demanding aspect of screen performance at some point or another. Of course, each film will bring its own challenges, a series of problems waiting to be solved. And they can be solved. You will solve them. That's your job!

Imagine working on a film entitled *The Really Dreadful Abominable Snowman*. The characters involved find themselves stranded on an isolated station at the North Pole. But we know the production cannot afford a trip to the chilly roof of the world, so it is all shot at Pinewood Studios. Weeks are spent on the exterior scenes. Styrofoam droplets are blown by giant wind machines into the faces of the cast, who do a marvellous job of lip-shivering even if outside this artificial environment it is the middle of summer.

With the exteriors in the can, the production company is ready to film the interior locations – maybe three months or more later. A set will have been built to represent the interior of the base camp. Happily, the continuity team will be on hand to remind you of the following:

- The order in which you entered the camp.
- What time of day/night you entered.
- What you were carrying.
- What you were wearing.
- How snow-covered you were.
- Whether your goggles were up or down.
- How your coat was buttoned.

But it is for you, the screen actor, to create and recreate the more specific emotional and physical continuity in which your character entered that base camp door.

- Were you carrying a prop? Gun? Spear? Walking stick? In which hand?
- Were the snow boots making your character limp? If so, which foot?
- Did you have frostbite? How many fingers? Which hand? (Or foot if toes?)
- How cold were you? Mildly discomforted? Freezing? Painfully ice-cubed?
- How was the death of your colleague, Fred, affecting you? Delighted to have his share of diminishing food stocks? Guilty because you survived and your friend didn't?
- How hungry were you? Peckish? Ravenous?

- How relieved are you to have escaped danger? Ecstatic? Visibly jubilant? Quietly contemplative?
- How tired are you? Slightly? Exhausted? Near death?
- In response to the line 'Where's Fred?', what is your character's response?
- How regretful were you for killing that Really Dreadful Abominable Snowman as an act of revenge for Fred's death – only to find you had killed the wrong (and wholly) innocent one, the friendly snowman. Awww!

In this example it is quite possible that the interior shoot might take place before the location shoot – and then you really *have* got to get your thought processes in order.

What is required of you is to be ready when called, and to deliver when asked; all in a calm and professionally collected manner. Let there be no panic! In *Alice in Wonderland* the White Rabbit's main characteristic is anxiety. He's always worried about being late and unprepared for whatever meeting or event he has to attend. He brings with him disorder, chaos, panic and self-doubt. *Don't be a White Rabbit!* His only plan is to continually move forward at a breathless pace in the vain hope that everything will be fine. Hope is good, but a good plan is better.

Take your map

It's not at all easy to maintain your sense of character continuity – unless you are well prepared and have planned thoroughly. Too late for the White Rabbit but let us help you plan better, think ahead and create a safety net. What you need is a map!

> A map does not just chart, it unlocks and formulates meaning; it forms bridges between here and there, between disparate ideas that we did not know were previously connected. (Reif Larson)[1]

---

[1]Reif Larsen, *The Selected Works of T. S. Spivet* (London: Penguin, 2009), review, Goodreads.com. Available at: https://www.goodreads.com/quotes/tag/maps [accessed 11 May 2019].

What's a map got to do with acting? Well, think about the challenges of working on different locations: perhaps even continents and sometimes over days, weeks or even months. You have a job that begins in early March, but the pick-up shots are called for late June. In between these two dates it is very possible that as an actor you might just work on another film, TV, radio or stage show. How will you ever remember what you were doing and the intensity with which you were doing it? What about how you *said* it? Revisiting previous performance can be a shock – and perhaps it should be:

> Then, suddenly, you're back in your old character. You see this completely strange person on the screen with funny hair and a moustache, and you think, God, how did I sound at that time? (Caine 1997: 81)

On the other hand, you have got to be able to find the vocal and physical life when you come back to the next day's shoot. Even if there are weeks between shoots, your character must be consistent. At the same time, you need to find the emotional pitch, which may be different from the previous scene or the next (or the other way round!). Get yourself a map. Maps in performance are not a recent invention. British stage and film actor Robert Donat (1905–58) created what he called an 'Emotion Chart' in the days when the ideas of Stanislavski were unknown in the West (see Figure 14). An example of his working methodology deals with his character development in *The Citadel* (King Vidor, 1938). Not easy to take in at first glance, the chart lists all the locations in chronological order and the graph line reflects Donat's emotional pitch through the shooting schedule. Some of the upper parts of the graph have been lost, but the chart is clearly designed to allow Donat to move from location to location and shot to shot, maintaining an emotional coherence.

Robert Donat's 'emotion chart' worked for him. It clearly denotes the inner feelings and outward situations of the character he created according to the given circumstances of *The Citadel* script, but, more importantly, it allows for visits/revisits to scenes about to be shot or reshot, or simply so that he can keep an eye on the various stages of emotional delivery.[2]

---

[2]For a full analysis of the Emotion Chart, see Lowe (2007).

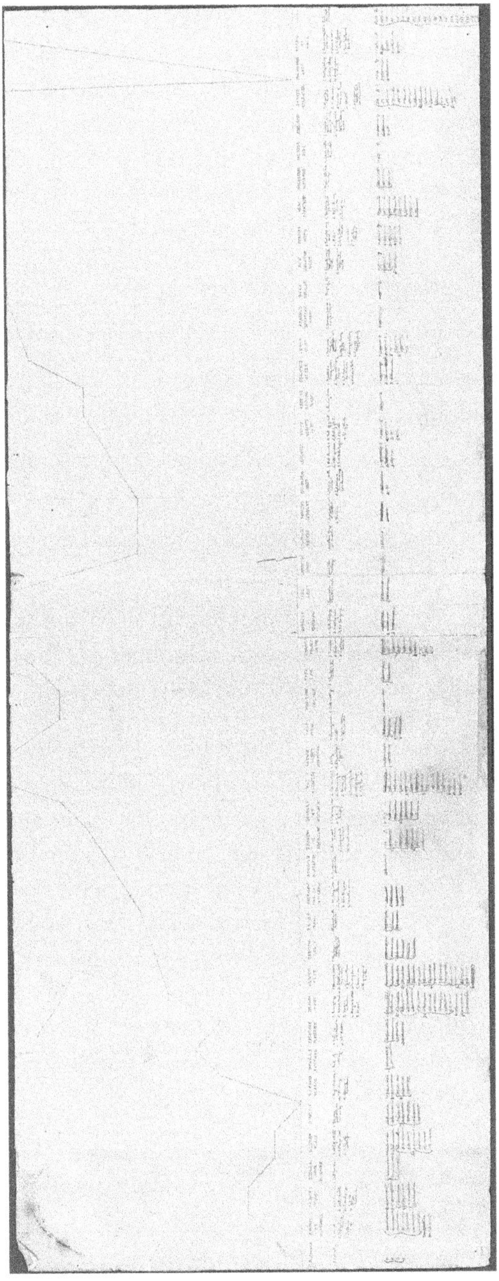

FIGURE 14 Robert Donat's Emotion Chart. Reproduced courtesy of the Donat family and copyright of the University of Manchester.

Jack Nicholson works on a script by breaking down each section into a number of 'beats and measures' that enable him to find the underlying rhythm before going into rehearsals.[3] We recommend that you too find a map that works for you: some way of charting your journey through the screenplay even when the journey is interrupted or diverted. Your own map will be personalized by necessity, depending on the demands of the screenplay, but a 'starter' map will be informed by:

- A study of the script over and over again.
- Your creation of the character's backstory (see Chapter 2).
- Getting used to making notes (always carry a back-pocket notebook and pen).
- Knowing where you are at each point – physically and emotionally.
- Carrying your 'map' throughout a shoot ready to guide you if you need it.
- Learning your lines. All of your lines in all of your scenes. The act of learning lines is the single contribution to the filmmaking process that you do control completely. Embrace it.

Let the writer's words map out the trajectory of the story and your character's part in it. Don't fall into the trap of thinking that you can upload them to your brain the night before the shoot and then recite them magnificently the next day, leading to an Oscar nomination for your troubles by the end of the week. It won't happen that way. The moment the script arrives through your letterbox, read it. Once you have the lines down, you won't have to worry about what a shoot throws your way. And throw it will.

Stay on top of everything right from the start. You don't want to be caught out in front of a full film crew having to turn to your fellow actor nervously whispering: 'Where were we?'

---

[3]Ron Rosenbaum, 'The Creative Mind; Acting: The Method and Mystique of Jack Nicholson', *New York Times*, 13 July 1986. Available at: https://www.nytimes.com/1986/07/13/magazine/the-creative-mind-acting-the-method-and-mystique-of-jack-nicholson.html [accessed 11 May 2019].

> The hardest thing about movie acting is that if you're playing a character who changes within the movie, you've got to do that, but you've got to do it out of sequence, because we never have gotten to shoot in sequence, and that's really, really tough. (John Sayles)[4]

Michael Caine recounts how he was caught out by a simple change in the weather whilst filming an exterior scene for *Kidnapped* (1972). The director, Delbert Mann, decided that because the sun was now shining brightly, after a rainy morning in the Scottish Highlands, he would take full advantage of the unscheduled natural lighting mood. He would shoot an entirely different sequence to the one planned. For Caine it happened to involve a two-page soliloquy that he hadn't yet learned. Luckily, he picks up dialogue fast and managed to save face by learning the scene as the shot was being set up by the crew. When action was called, Caine performed the speech perfectly in one take and without a single missed word or beat. Impressive. But what is the lesson here? For Caine, that type of near disaster would never happen again: from then on he would always arrive on the set prepared for any change in sequencing, recall or new direction; he would always know his lines from first day of shoot to last.

> Learn your lines for the whole film before you start shooting, and keep studying them during the gaps in your shooting. (Caine 1997: 26)

> *"I once worked as an actor on a long-forgotten TV series called* Inside *(RTE, 1985–6) playing a prison officer. He popped in and out of episodes mostly when strong-arm techniques were required during prison breaks and altercations – and there were a lot of those! I realized that I was constantly carrying around large reams of paper that contained the scenes, times, calls etc. I worked out that most of the scenes of the story didn't involve my prison officer, so I took a pair of scissors and cut out the ones that he was involved in*

[4]Quoted on BrainyQuote.com. Available at: https://www.brainyquote.com/quotes/john_sayles_270707?src=t_sequence [accessed 11 May 2019].

and then pasted them in an order that allowed for a chronological character arc. By seeing the script in this way, it gave me a mental picture of my character's story. I could map out his emotional state in relation to any other character who was in the scene and would simply have to look at the redesigned script to know exactly what was required of the character. The map worked, no matter what order the sequences were shot in. – Paul Conway, actor

Mapping means the piecing together of the little things to ultimately reveal the bigger emotional picture. Look at the script. The writer has her own map, placing plot points as markers for the director and actors to follow. Directions, indicators and maps are all around us. We use them to help us start a journey and to locate the destination point. In acting terms, a character map functions as a tool to:

- Connect actions – in *Klute* (Alan J. Pakula, 1971) the character Bree Daniels connects her past to her present via conversations with her psychiatrist.
- Build on previous actions – the character Rocky Graziano becomes a successful professional boxer but appears, through the obvious aggression, to be fighting his past, in *Somebody Up There Likes Me* (Robert Wise, 1956).
- Contribute to later actions – a character called Harmonica maps out his future from the result of a single, destructive action witnessed when he was a young boy, in *Once Upon a Time in the West* (Sergio Leone, 1968).
- Help with looping – if re-recording or dubbing post-production is required, your map can be an essential aid in ensuring that we cannot see the joins!

Looping is the filmmaking term for dubbing, mixing or re-recording in post-production. It is the process by which new vocal recordings are mixed with the original material for technical or artistic reasons.

As your career develops, you will find your own way of mapping, but here's a straightforward approach that might get you started. Look at your script. Write down all of your character's emotional plot points in a straight line for every scene or episode. Or use index cards. Include one or two sentences of information about what your character is experiencing at each point. Then write on another card for the next point and so on. Whatever your choice of mapping, do remember to keep it with you at all times during filming so that you can access it easily. Know your character, know your script. Preparation is a major advantage. For the film actor it can:

- minimize possible problems
- maximize time-saving
- showcase your professionalism.

And such professionalism might just get you a part in the director's next film, *The Really,* Really *Dreadful Abominable Snowman: Not Dead Yeti.*

Superobjective

Your map serves as both a technical guide through the jungle of the shoot and an emotional guide, which naturally brings us back to the previously discussed notion of the 'superobjective'. You, the actor, need to have an awareness of the character's complete story arc – whilst, of course, playing the immediate objectives in each contributing scene. Knowing the trajectory of the character's whole story will allow you to plot the stopping places on the route. The superobjective is given to you by what happens to the character over the whole story, and you have to make logical sense of the emotions and actions to fit with the dénouement. You may be familiar with Charles Dickens's novel *Great Expectations*. You may not be aware that the novel has two endings. The best known is the one in which Pip and Estella are eventually reconciled and was written to please the public, who wanted a happy ending. The original (which many regard as being more truthful to the psychological structure of the book) sees them destined to remain apart. If you were an actor playing either of these roles, you would have to mould your objectives and motivations throughout the story towards one of these distinct endings to ensure coherence. Having a 'map' or some sort of personal emotion graph will help you moderate this journey to a coherent conclusion.

Films that deliberately experiment with timelines such as *Once Upon a Time in the West*, *Groundhog Day* (Harold Ramis, 1993) or *Pulp Fiction* (Quentin Tarantino, 1994) present their own challenges. The screen actor needs to have a detailed understanding of where the character is emotionally and physically when revisiting a story thought to be finished. It can be confusing. How do we get back into the feeling of the scene? Where were we?

The *Star Trek* diversion

In Chapter 4 we considered the act of 'keeping it real'. But how do we keep it real over a longer period of time with a break – or several – in between? Let's look at this through two examples of the same scene under construction. Imagine you are cast as a crewmember of the Starship *Enterprise*. This imaginary *Star Trek* storyline involves a heated conversation about how to defeat the Klingons and save planet Earth – again. Once a decision has been made by Captain Kirk, your character (insert name here), Dr McCoy and Spock embark on a deadly deep-space mission. Here is the scene as presented on screen:

- The crew enter the Transporter Room.
- After an engineer twirls a few dials, the crew dematerialize and are beamed down to Planet Alpha 177.
- Once rematerialized on Planet Alpha 177, a desolate, uninhabitable wasteland, the crew pinpoint a geographical position emitting a signal. But who from?
- The crew look at each other in wonderment.
- They trundle precariously through a radioactive storm so intense that one of them drops dead. Sorry, but it has to be your character; the other three are on long-term contracts! You should never have put on the red T-shirt.

The scene as shot:

- 18 December (all day), an exterior building site somewhere in the Hollywood Hills standing in for Planet Alpha 177. The storm is shot here with atmospheric giant wind machines, this time blowing radioactive droplets into the faces of the actors. Don't worry, talcum powder will probably be used instead of radioactive material. But are you allergic? (See Chapter 11).

- 19 December (morning), an interior studio shot of the crew entering the Transporter Room looking very apprehensive. Close-ups all round.
- 19 December (afternoon), an interior studio shot of the crew looking at each other in wonderment at the incoming signal. Close-ups all round.
- 20 December (morning), at the moment of expiration, the character reaches out in great emotional turmoil towards the alien signal before hitting the ground.
- Lunch.
- 20 December (afternoon), a close-up of your face (welcome back from the dead) looking puzzled because you are holding the alien signal detector as it pings.
- 21 December (morning), a close-up of your character pointing towards the alien signal before resting forever on the blowing sands of Alpha 177.
- WRAP!

Dramatic scenes in the can, the shoot is over. The crew might remain on site to film other scenes in the same or nearby locations. In addition, they may possibly record some ambient sound from the location, untainted by actors, that can be added to the final edit. The screen actors now have some time off. Unfortunately for your character, this will be a lot of time off.

Not easy jumping from one location to another – interior, exterior, then back to interior, or was that exterior? What about filming a death scene, then filming an earlier one where your character is very much alive. Difficult? Beam me up, Scotty!

It's a very demanding aspect of filmmaking, but how does one respond to these demands? Maps work. Use them. Create one that suits you. By preparing yourself ahead of time, you'll find that the problems will disappear before they have a chance to interfere with your work.

To the tutor

Students will to a greater or lesser extent be accustomed to ideas of working from a backstory to develop a superobjective in their theatre work. They will also perhaps be adept at identifying their motivations and objectives in each of their scenes and interactions. For the reasons outlined in this chapter, screen work presents a host of additional challenges. They are unlikely to even meet all the other actors in the production and teamwork can feel tentative at best. The frequent stops and starts, the delays and non-chronological shooting schedule can be a real barrier to presenting a coherent performance. The very fact of moving between location and studio set can be disorientating. The theatrical security of going 'out there' and giving a well-rehearsed performance is nought but a satisfying dream! The exercises that follow will give your students some experience of working with these challenges and help them draw their own maps. (See also Chapter 2 on backstory.)

EXERCISE 8:1 LIFE STORY IN SIX PICTURES

Each actor chooses a role from any play or screenplay and creates a series of six 'stills' which tell the character's story. The rest of the group have to try to identify the story or describe it. They can ask to see the stills again *in any order* to help them!

EXERCISE 8:2 MAFIA MAP

The group could try this viewing/discussion exercise as a way of exploring emotional continuity. Suggest they watch *The Godfather* together, considering the narrative from the character Kay's point of view. What would her map look like? Create a backstory for her and then a map or emotion chart for her progress through the story. Relate this to her superobjective and her specific motivations and objectives in each of her scenes.

EXERCISE 8:3 TIME WARP

Here is an exercise that groups of actors can try to help develop an ability to work without a chronological structure. It does not require a camera so can be planned outside the workshop sessions:

Ask the actors to prepare (improvise and then script) three short scenes that tell a story chronologically. For example:

- Planning a heist – carrying out the heist – the aftermath of the heist.
- Falling in love – being in love – splitting up.
- Being new parents – being parents of a teenager – teenager leaving home (illustrated in Figure 15).
- Getting a promotion – working ten years later – being made redundant.
- A group of contented friends – one dealing with mental illness – situation 'resolves'.

FIGURE 15 Exercise 8:3 Time warp. Photo by Abby Timms.

The scenes should make a range of emotional demands on the actors, which should be 'mapped'. Backstories need to be discussed and decided. Avoid any 'prima donna-ism': how the group deals with the mental illness of a friend is as interesting and important as the portrayal of the victim of the condition.

You can then 'play' these three scenes in any order, even 'fast-forwarding' and 'rewinding' so that the actors can practise quickly 'pitching in' to the appropriate emotional state for their characters. The results can be recorded for further analysis and the 'game' replayed in the light of these observations. The actors will learn to quickly adopt the appropriate mental state and to be able to go from nought to sixty in a heartbeat!

Different screen actors will have their individual coping strategies when it comes to this need to be ready to jump back into the scene physically and emotionally at a moment's notice. Let them find what works. But they need to have these tools. Insist on backstories and a map!

EXERCISE 8:4 THE 'TELL-TALE HEART' (AFTER EDGAR ALLAN POE)

Finding freedom on a shoot can be difficult but it does come with practice – and the best practice is making film (something which we look at in greater detail in Chapter 10). With that in mind we have added a script here that may be fun for your students to shoot. The normal directions for a screenplay have been removed, leaving just the bare bones. This is so the cohort can put the film together under your direction with full artistic ownership. The story takes place on a movie set and the students will play a cast and crew making a film. The storyline explains itself, but students will have to create a backstory and a character map, and the film needs to be shot out of sequence to get the full benefit of non-linear shooting.

(Everything is in place. Camera and crew ready. Lenore Poe is sitting in a large armchair.)

Director	Action!
Lenore Poe	It wasn't what was seen, it was what he alone could hear. He … aw!
Director	And the problem now is?
Lenore Poe	It's my character. I'm playing Edgar Allan Poe's daughter. Poe never had a daughter!
Director	It's an … ad-ap-tation!
Lenore Poe	But I'm a classically trained actress! I seek realism! I have worked with Ross Kemp!
Director	And I've worked with … (to cameraperson) is the camera still running? Why is the camera still running?
Cameraperson	You didn't call cut! Last week you gave me a lecture for calling cut when the actress moved out of frame!
Lenore Poe	And my costume doesn't fit!
Costume (stepping in)	I've bent over backwards to comply with your demands.
Make-up (stepping in)	And by the way, Miss Sarah Bernhardt, I spend hours every morning applying make-up to your character, as designed by you, only to have you wipe it off every time you feel like it, and to add insult to my misery you go and apply your own Boots Mascara 666.
Boom operator	My arms are killing me!
Director	Well lower the boom then!
Cameraperson	You haven't called cut!

Boom operator	Yeah, you haven't called cut! And by the way, you gave me a lecture yesterday for lowering the boom too early!
Director	Because you ruined the shot!
Boom operator	She was mumbling. If I'd stuck my ear down her throat, I still wouldn't have been able to figure out what she was saying!
Lenore Poe	I'm a classically trained actress.
Producer (stepping in)	Cut!
Director	You can't call cut! You're the producer! Only the director can call cut and I'm the director.
All	Call cut then!
Director (sheepishly)	Cut!
Producer	Happy? Now, let me make it all so clear. I hire the talent. I pay the wage. I bought the script. I do the firing. (beat) The talent sells the picture. I chose well. She's a classically trained actress *and* she's worked with Ross Kemp. Need I say more? (calm) All great talented people are infested with problems. Haven't you seen the *Apocalypse Now* documentary? Let's clear the set for a break, after which we shall return to our magical journey into our little world of Poe and his thankfully out-of-copyright works. Now … clear the set!

(Everybody clears the set. Edgar Allan Poe appears from nowhere and steps in front of the camera.)

Edgar Allan Poe (stepping in from shadows)	I am Edgar Allan Poe, 1809 to 1849. A most extraordinary writer, raconteur and … (begins to cry) I can't allow any more

bad adaptations of my work. Nobody will ever kill my work again. No more so-called adaptations. *The Tell-Tale Heart* will seek revenge. I am Edgar Allan Poe and I'm coming to get you, starting with the producer, then the director, then, well, let's face it, *you are all . . . !*

Fin

FIGURE 16 Exercise 8:4 Tutor setting up a scene for *The Tell-Tale Heart*. Photo by Abby Timms.

Screen performances to consider

Although extremely rare, some film productions are the exception to the rule when it comes to out-of-sequence shooting. The director Sebastian Schipper shot *Victoria* (2010) in one continuous take, totalling 138 minutes. Aleksandr Sokurov created *Russian Ark* (2002) in a single shot with a runtime of 99 minutes. Clear, linear and very attractive for the actors involved in delivering the performances, but that approach wouldn't work for every film. Imagine trying to shoot a *Star Trek* epic in one take? 'Illogical, Jim,' as Spock would say to Captain James Tiberius Kirk.

David Lean's epic film *Ryan's Daughter* (1970), a love story set against a political background, required many of the scenes to be staged on a beach, complete with either sunshine or storm conditions. The beach chosen was located on the west coast of Ireland in a place called Dingle. Unfortunately, the powers above the clouds had not read the script, so when sunshine was required storms appeared. Likewise, when storms were required sunshine appeared. All of this at a time of year when the chances of predicting the weather in that area would be akin to winning the lottery – twice in one week! Heavy rain and intermittent thunderstorms meant that for much of the scheduled time the cast and crew were hanging around. They were doing absolutely nothing at a big cost to the producers (MGM). Eventually, waiting for the right conditions was no longer an option. The production moved to the more predictable climes of South Africa. Shooting of the required scenes resumed after a long and very expensive search for a sandy beach sufficiently resembling the original one back in Ireland. They found one – Noordhoek Beach. In fact, if you watch the film, it is difficult to tell the difference between the two. When the South African shots were in the can (finished), the production moved back to Ireland. Amongst all that, the actors involved in the various productions referenced above, had to maintain a sense of reality in regard to their characters. If you take into consideration the delays or retakes and watch (or rewatch) the films mentioned, we would challenge you find a break in the concentration of any of the actors involved. Not even a flicker will betray the process they undertook as part of their contribution to the filmmaking experience. The actors rose above the interruptions, constant set-ups and demands. They maintained character. They *kept it real* by understanding the switch-on, switch-off element that film performance demands. They did their job.

Consider also the following films where the shooting conditions were extreme, where exterior shots were taken on location and mixed with interior studio shots, creating 'where were we?' moments for the actors.

- *Way Down East* (D. W. Griffith, 1920)
- *Trapeze* (Carol Reed, 1956)
- *The Naked Prey* (Cornel Wilde, 1965)
- *7 Women* (John Ford, 1966)

- *Ice Station Zebra* (John Sturges, 1968)
- *The Poseidon Adventure* (Ronald Neame, 1972)
- *The Shining* (Stanley Kubrick, 1980)
- *Death Hunt* (Peter Hunt, 1981)
- *Fargo* (Joel Coen and Ethan Coen (uncredited), 1996)
- *The Revenant* (Alejandro G. Iñárritu, 2015)

Screen Actors' Motto #8:
Your backstory is your starting point: follow your map to your destination.

9 IT'S GOOD TO CHEAT

Nothing is impossible. The word itself says I'M POSSIBLE.

ATTRIBUTED TO AUDREY HEPBURN[1]

To the actor

Let's be clear from the outset: 'cheating' is a term used both in theatre and screen recording. It is a good thing! In the proscenium theatre, to take a simple example, we watch the actors through the invisible fourth wall. They play their parts and direct their dialogue towards this invisible wall and we, the audience, accept that. In rehearsals actors may be asked to move a little more downstage in order to give the scene a more pleasing visual balance. It looks and feels 'right' within the theatrical conventions. In the recording studio 'cheating' is jargon for those adjustments that have to be made to what the actors or the camera are doing to ensure that it looks 'right' on screen. Having considered the distinctiveness of the screen actor's art, in this chapter we turn our attention in more detail to the technical challenges that this discipline has to adapt to on the studio floor. You are ready to produce a finely honed performance, but now you have to cope with the demands of blocking and camera angles, and respond to a myriad of artistic demands from the director and technical demands from the camera and sound crew.

In film and television production, to give the final product verisimilitude requires a lot of 'cheating'. Some of this merely affects the environment within which you have to perform. The kitchen cabinets may be slightly scaled down to 'look right' on screen. Light switches may

---

[1]Quoted on Goodreads.com. Available at: https://www.goodreads.com/quotes/12732-nothing-is-impossible-the-word-itself-says-i-m-possible [accessed 25 July 2018].

not be practical (i.e. functional). A studio set will lack walls and a ceiling, and food (aside from that which has to be eaten) will be sprayed and painted so that it presents the required visual effect and survives the heat from the lights.

Other aspects of this 'cheating' will require you to employ the various skills that have been outlined in the previous chapters. Obvious examples are driving a car, which, if being filmed on location, requires a particularly strong ability to concentrate whilst acting and driving safely. If driving in a studio set-up against a back projection or green screen, the challenge is to keep the situation real for us by responding to the road (imagined or projected on the screen) and, please, at least *glancing occasionally* at where you are going!

Some of our best-known actors have had huge 'cheating' demands made upon them. As mentioned in Chapter 3, Ian McKellen found *The Hobbit: An Unexpected Journey* a confusing experience and the challenges of performing to green screen too arduous, and came close to walking out of the film. He became very frustrated at endlessly performing solo and having to leave the interactions between Gandalf and the hobbits to be assembled digitally in post-production. It apparently took all Jackson's powers of persuasion to get McKellen to stay on the project.[2] On a talk show McKellen recalled:

> Some of it was really exciting like filming on a mountain top. But filming with a green screen is the miserable part … At the end of the first day, I shed a tear and with my head in my hand said, 'This is not why I became an actor,' forgetting the mikes were still on![3]

Your job is to help the audience/viewer to suspend their disbelief and accept the situation presented. In proscenium theatre we know that the three remaining walls are painted flats but our belief and enjoyment is disturbed if they flap when the door is slammed. In film it is generally true that much greater care is taken to ensure that the artifice is hidden, and the actor is key to creating this illusion. An example was given in

---

[2]Brian Boone, 'Scenes That Pushed Actors Too Far', Looper.com. Available at: http://www.looper.com/10058/scenes-almost-caused-actors-quit/ [accessed 3 June 2018]).

[3]Antonia Molly, 'Ian McKellen on Filming The Hobbit', *The Independent*, December 2014. Available at: http://www.independent.co.uk/arts-entertainment/films/news/ian-mckellen-on-filming-the-hobbit-i-had-no-idea-what-i-was-doing-9905416.html [accessed 3 June 2018].

Chapter 4 concerning the consumption of drinks on set. You have to make us believe that the liquid in the vessel is whisky, or coffee or beer or cola. No respectable director will allow alcohol on the set (far too dangerous after the eighth take!). The continuity team will have to ensure that the levels in the glasses or bottles are consistent with the previous action, but it is the actor's job to ensure that she drinks in the same way and at the same point in each take, be it a long, medium or close-up shot. Fluctuating liquid levels and inconsistent drinking patterns would present a nightmare for the editor to work around. The same applies to any aspect of the scene where consumable items are involved. Meals can present particular challenges for the whole production team, including the actors, as can those accursed cigarettes that change length from take to take! Let us consider some of the specific challenges for the screen actor where 'cheating' might be required, and offer some exercises that will help prepare you for the shoot.

Making it artificial to make it real

There is a great deal of artifice in the creation of film and television as there is in the creation of theatre. In theatre however, the audience are more ready, whilst suspending their disbelief, to acknowledge a wide range of genres, styles and actor/audience relationships. The artifice is part of the language of theatre and a significant part of its joy. Latterly at least, film has become primarily focused on presenting a pseudo-reality. Characters are expected to be people that we might well meet (though we might not want to!). To create this reality for the screen-watchers, filmmakers and screen actors have to employ a wide range of artifice that, in the end, we do not want the viewer to be aware of. We lie and cheat to be truthful. In this process you need to trust the director and the editor. And you need to help the cameraperson, for example by keeping your actions consistent from take to take and avoiding unplanned movements that might be impossible for the camera to track – especially in close-up. A small movement of the hands on the arms of the chair (for example) to indicate that you are about to jump to your feet might help the cameraperson keep up with you. Otherwise, you will leap out of frame and the scene will have to be reshot. For each take, you need to perform the action at the same point else you will receive the curses of both camera operator and editor. Also you might bang your head on the boom mic!

Artistically, the director is the only person with a full grasp of the overall project and she will work with the editor to solidify that vision. What ends up on the screen is, for the viewer, the only 'truth' and it is your job to make that truth believable (in each and every take); to make us believe that you have trekked across Antarctica and found refuge in a warm base camp, even if you have in fact spent two days stomping around a Tunisian desert and ended up three months later in a deserted warehouse on an out-of-town industrial estate.

To the tutor

We have included more exercises in this chapter than in any other. The reason for this is straightforward: most of the acting skills we discuss are developments and specific applications of the skills of any form of acting. How to interact with the technology of screen recording and its potential pitfalls, however, tend to be less considered by training regimes. The language of screen is different from the language of theatre,[4] and these exercises are designed to help the actor become competent and confident in their interaction with the camera.

EXERCISE 9:1 YOU'RE SITTING ON MY LAP

This exercise demonstrates that to make a physical interrelationship between characters look natural on screen, it is often necessary to require the actors to adopt very unnatural positions.

Get two actors to sit at a table as they would to have a normal conversation over a cup of coffee. Ask the camera operator to shoot them in long shot and then slowly zoom in to a tight two-shot. It will become clear that what even initially seems a somewhat awkward distance between the actors appears increasingly unnatural as

---

[4]By 'the language of the screen' and the 'language of theatre', we do not refer to the jargon of the shoot, but to the way that each of these art forms communicates: the combination of acting, technology (sound and lighting), design, direction and, in the case of recorded material, editing.

the shot gets tighter. You will end up with a very unsatisfactory shot composition. In fact, what such a shot conveys, and what the viewer will be expecting, is the imminent appearance of a third actor to take up the central vacuum and make a three-shot. Exactly the same principle applies if the experiment is undertaken by actors standing in conversation. The natural, polite distance we leave between ourselves and others when talking looks vast on the screen.

Now, exactly how close we stand to someone when talking will be determined by a range of factors. How well do we know them or want to know them? Is the environment noisy? (the ambient sound may be added post-production). What is the nature of the relationship? These and other circumstances will have been considered by the actors as part of their preparation, but here on the set or on location it is not enough that the situation is believable; it has to be believable on the screen. And whilst it may seem more 'real' to the actors to face each other directly when talking, the lighting and camera angle may demand that they 'cheat' this to a slight diagonal so that reactions are caught sufficiently by the camera. Often this spatial orientation will need to be varied from shot to shot. More distance is acceptable in a long shot and less in a head-and-shoulders two-shot. Actors have to keep it real, not anticipate (see Chapter 4) and present the performance for the first time every time. And no matter how you think it went, what is on the screen is the only truth.

This can be practised in a workshop situation. The participants, looking solely at the screen, can direct the actors to adjust their proximity until they are satisfied that it looks 'right'. On turning back to observe the live actors, you may be surprised at how close they are. They may have had to intertwine the legs of the chairs, or one may even have had to put a leg across that of his fellow actor. If you are hardened criminals discussing a heist, this may test your skills of concentration and belief in the moment-to-moment truth of the scene! Figure 17 illustrates this conundrum. In the first shot the actors seem well placed for a conversation – perhaps in a café. The second shot, taken from a distance, shows just how close together they had to be to make the first shot look 'right' on screen.

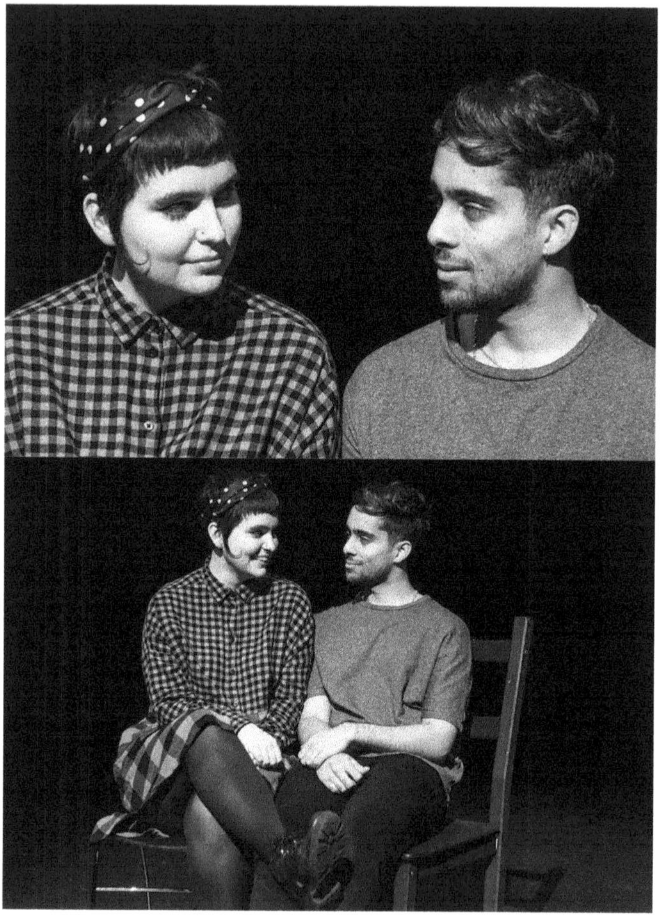

FIGURE 17 Exercise 9:1 Cheating positions: you're sitting on my lap. Photo by Abby Timms.

This simple exercise can also be used to practise finding your marks (see following exercise) by walking into the scene and sitting or standing. If the shot is tight, it will be important to hit your mark accurately.

EXERCISE 9:2 ON YOUR MARKS: GETTING TO THE RIGHT PLACE AND STAYING THERE

In the theatre, actors have a certain amount of lassitude when it comes to being in the right place on stage. Often it is not crucial to be standing in exactly the rehearsed spot. Neither will it usually matter if we choose to move, on impulse, earlier or later than in other performances. This is part of the living spontaneity of theatre that contributes to its power. Of course, there may be specials or lighting effects that demand the actor is exactly in the agreed spot, and occasions when it is vital that she has 'found her light' lest she leaves herself in shadow. It may even be so crucial that the floor is marked to aid the actor. At the end of this chapter we cite the example of Spencer Tracy, who was at times quite blatant about finding his mark. We don't recommend this as an approach for today's actors.

For the screen actor the discipline is always much tighter. The camera is going to be looking at you far more closely than the theatre audience, who are free to take in the whole stage scene. On screen a few centimetres can make the difference between being in or out of frame or focus. In close-up it will be important that the actor moves hardly at all. They may have to keep on their mark and be aware of the range of movement they have at their disposal. This can be checked with the director, AD or camera operator.

'Finding your mark' means coming into shot and stopping at the right point to satisfy the needs of the composition as planned by the director and anticipated by the camera operator. In a studio setting this 'mark' may well be a piece of tape on the floor, though don't expect it to be brightly coloured. Especially on exterior locations, the 'mark' will be a sand-filled hessian sausage, though in all cases the eye of the camera will determine if a mark can be used. If a mark cannot be accommodated, the actor has to become adept at judging the distance they are walking and locating the desired position perhaps by reference to furniture, equipment, marks in the pavement or lamp posts. This sounds quite a daunting prospect, but skills in this respect can be learned by becoming more aware of the power of peripheral vision:

- The actors stand in a circle and look straight ahead. Ask them to make themselves aware of how much they are able to see of those standing to their right and left and how much they can discern of what is above them and on the floor even without moving their eyes. Get the actors to describe what they see and to note any movements they observe from those around them.
- Using the camera, set up a tight two-shot with two actors. Allow them to take it in turns to walk into the correct position. Then try this using a 'mark' – a piece of tape on the floor. Will they stand with their toes on it? Their heels? A foot either side? They need to be consistent in each take. They should practise finding this mark without looking directly at it – using their peripheral vision. Figure 18 shows the actor approaching the mark, which he has to 'hit' without looking directly at it.

FIGURE 18 Exercise 9:2 On your marks: getting to the right place and staying there. Photo by Abby Timms.

- In this version the camera follows the actor walking the length of the room until they reach their mark, by which time they will be in close-up. Ask them to find this position without looking at the floor. Then get them to do this whilst reciting a section of text (or a nursery rhyme), trying to time the walk so that they stop on the mark as they deliver the last line.

"The camera lens is the eyeline you work with, so if you need to be looking to the left or the right of camera, use the lens as your guide and not the size of the room. Everything is made larger through the lens, so don't use the room as your eyeline. Stick close to the lens! – Debbie Bridge, actor

EXERCISE 9:3 IS THERE ANYBODY THERE? WORKING WITHOUT THE OTHER ACTORS

From cheating spatial relationships, we turn in this exercise to having to work with actors who are not there. A particular shot may, for example, require the recipient of the line to be absent to allow the camera to obtain the desired angle. The dialogue may be fed in from nearby or may be absent altogether, which will require the actor to respond 'as if' the feed line had been delivered. For the theatre actor there will always be someone to bounce your performance off, but frequently when shooting a scene you may be acting alone. You may be acting opposite an actor who is on another continent, or who has gone to the bar, or you may be staring into the eyes of a savage monster that will be CGI-ed into the scene later. Such requirements make huge demands of the screen actor's mastery of all his screen acting skills. In Figure 19 an actor addresses his lines to a second actor who is not present, taking care to avoid looking straight into the lens of the camera.

FIGURE 19 Exercise 9:3 Is there anybody there? Working without the other actors. Photo by Abby Timms.

For these exercises it is helpful if actors have memorized a section of script. First of all, shoot the scene in a head-and-shoulders two-shot. Then, for the close-ups, remove one of the actors and replace him with the camera. Note that usually the actor being shot should not look into the lens of the camera but to an appropriate eyeline to the side of the camera (see Exercise 9:4). There are several challenges here for the actor:

1. Working without the visual clues from the fellow actor. Listening and responding will have been established in the previous takes, and now the actor must employ them from memory.
2. As this is a close-up shot, the camera will be searching out any inconsistencies – including the focus of the eye.
3. Lines may be being fed to the actor from a different location than the one the actor is speaking and reacting to. This must not be allowed to distract.

Variations on Exercise 9:3. If facilities permit, this exercise can be tried out using other camera angles (paying appropriate attention to health and safety please!):

- The actor could be up a ladder talking to another character above her, the camera standing in for the second actor.
- The actor can try talking to a (not-present) child (with the camera providing the child's POV).
- The actor could interact with a monster (of whatever height – or even of varying height). Text here can be minimal but might include a lot of screaming!

EXERCISE 9:4 FANCY A QUICKIE?

This one really is a quickie. Challenge your actors to play any scene or moment and to steal a momentary glance into the lens of the camera without it being noticed. Can't be done? That is how sensitive the camera is to what is going on.

EXERCISE 9:5 THE EYES HAVE IT: EYELINES AND EYE FOCUS

In Exercise 9:3 we mentioned that the camera can be unforgiving if both the direction and the focus of the eyes are not correct. This exercise is about practising the direction of the eyeline and controlling the eyes' focus.

Whether in a studio or on location, agreeing with the director and fellow actors on the location of whatever you are looking at is going to be important. If the character is sitting with a friend in a room and both glance at the non-existent TV set, it will disturb the viewer if they look in, even slightly, different directions. Encourage your actors to choose a spot on the wall, on the lighting stand, on a monitor, that can stand in for the 'clock' or the TV, or whatever.

By doing this they not only have an agreed angle for the glance, but an agreed distance. Especially in close-up, it can be very clear how far away the thing is that a character is looking at. Whenever possible it helps to have a fixed object on which to focus. If, as in the previous exercises, you are playing to an actor who is not there, choose a point on the camera equipment. Check with the director, AD or camera operator what looks right.

There may be occasions, however, when none of these techniques is possible and the actor may have to control the focus of their eyes and fight against their natural tendency to adjust. This is something screen actors can practise on their own. Take a piece of paper with some writing or an image on it. Hold the paper at the distance you would normally hold it to focus on it. Then try to maintain that focus whilst removing the paper. Similarly, try looking at something at a distance, across the street or on the horizon, and then interpose a piece of paper, or ask someone to stand in the line of vision, again whilst trying to maintain that long focus. Get actors to practise altering their focus, stopping at will from close to long and back again. Let them stop when they start to get a headache!

> People don't always express their inner thoughts to one another; a conversation may be quite trivial, but often the eyes will reveal what a person really thinks or feels. (Alfred Hitchcock, quoted in Comey 2002: 16)

Note: Actors will very rarely be required to look straight into the lens of the camera. This 'says' a very particular thing – that I am talking directly to you, the individual viewer. It was famously used by director Lewis Gilbert in directing Michael Caine in *Alfie* (1966) and has occasionally been used in film and television since. It is, perhaps, the screen equivalent of the theatrical 'aside', now seldom seen in contemporary productions other than pantomime. In most screen productions it remains a rare convention and will nearly always be seen as an actor's error, to be followed by the dreaded words 'Cut! Reset! Let's go again', though often you will see film extras getting away with what they suppose to be a casual glance at the camera. It is rather like waving to mum and dad whilst performing in the school play!

See also Exercise 9:7 for similar exercises for voice levels.

EXERCISE 9:6 LOOK AT ME AND SAY THAT

In a close-up, when addressing another person, it will become apparent which eye we are focusing on – or rather, it will become very apparent that our gaze or focus is jumping from one eye to the other. Try having a conversation at close quarters, looking each other in the eye, and note how there is a natural tendency to flit from eye to eye. On screen this is distracting. Choose an eye and keep to it. It also helps if this eye is the one nearest the camera. Try this short improvisation to test this control, though you could also use many of the other dialogues and exercises in these chapters. The scene should be shot 'over the shoulder' twice – once for each actor. It doesn't matter if the dialogue in the second version varies from the first; what we are observing is the focus of the eyes. Actors should concentrate on keeping their focus fixed and not allowing themselves to glance at the camera (the cardinal sin!).

Improv 1

(A is sitting at a restaurant table. B joins them and sits down.)

A. Why are you never here?

B. I am here.

(The improv continues until one or other of the characters leaves. They must have a motivation for leaving. Set a rough time limit on the scene, but it should continue until the director says 'Cut!')

Improv 2

(A is sitting in an armchair. He has a blanket over his knees. B enters, pulling up another, lighter, chair and begins.)

B. I want to hold you.

A. Who are you?

(The improv continues until the director says 'Cut!' There may be no need for either actor to leave the scene.)

Variation on Exercise 9:5. Once the scene is established, trying playing it as a romcom, a drama, a soap opera or a sitcom.

Note: It will be clear that many of the skills discussed in previous chapters are – or should be – involved in this scene. If fruitful, you may even wish to script the scene and use it more extensively, applying not only the skills discussed in this chapter but also those concerning keeping it real, not anticipating and building a belief in when and where the actors are. If you apply this exercise to the continuity challenges considered in Chapter 8, the actors can practise carrying over the emotional pitch of their work from week to week.

EXERCISE 9:7 TURN THE SOUND DOWN: I CAN'T HEAR MYSELF ACT!

(Note: This exercise requires a facility for playing back the recorded material with music added.)

Another situation that screen actors are invariably required to cope with is a scene set in a club or other noisy social environment. This presents technical problems for the sound technicians and the editor, especially when diegetic sound is involved. It would be impossible to maintain the integrity of this background ambient sound whilst cutting between takes. For this reason ambient sound is usually inserted post-production. As a result, actors will be required to employ their own emotion memories to recreate a conversational style appropriate to a noisy nightclub whilst actually performing in a quietened studio or location setting. This can feel extremely odd, even though it is an experience we all share and to which we can all relate. The starting point here may well be observation – of oneself and others in a real situation. Actors should note how, in real life, in a noisy environment, they direct their speech at the other person's ears: how they overarticulate and exaggerate the movements of their mouths. They might also demonstrate how much effort and concentration they are putting into communicating by screwing up their faces, tilting their heads to help the speaker and brushing the hair away from their ears. Above all, actors need to become aware of how loudly one has to speak, and then file that away neatly in their memory.

As a group the training actors can then try recording conversations in such environments (whilst others perhaps dance in the background to the silence!) and then review them with and without music overlaid.

Screen performances to consider

It is said that one day Humphrey Bogart was recalled to the set of *Casablanca* (Michael Curtiz, 1942) to reshoot a moment that had been missed off the shot list. It is the scene when the German soldiers break into a rendition of a patriotic German song, 'The Watch on the Rhine'. In response, the patrons of Rick's Bar respond with a passionate version of the French national anthem, the Marseillaise. Perhaps it was an afterthought, but Curtiz clearly decided that this defiance, even encouraged by Lazlo, was implausible without the permission of the bar's owner, Rick. Anyway, Bogart was recalled to the set, asked to stand in the bar, with just a few extras in the background, and nod. During this recording the band was not there. The German soldiers were not there. The tear-stained French sympathizers were not there. All that was required was the physical presence and the eyeline and the nod. That nod appears in the final cut as a sign to the band that they should play the Marseillaise and, as such, it becomes one of the most significant moments in the film: where Rick finally takes sides.[5]

Spencer Tracy, in the opinion of Michael Caine, can always be seen finding his mark:

> In a Tracy movie, he walks in, looks straight down at his mark, finds it, looks up and speaks. It became the Spencer Tracy style. Look for it: Tracy looking up at the camera and speaking. Gave him a sort of sincerity … but he was just a bloke looking for his mark.[6]

---

[5]'Casablanca La Marseillaise', YouTube.com, uploaded by CortoMaltese86, 6 October 2009. Available at: https://www.youtube.com/watch?v=HM-E2H1ChJM [accessed 25 July 2018].

[6]Roger Ebert, 'Michael Caine: Doing Something with Nothing', RogerEbert.com, 27 July 1980. Available at: http://www.rogerebert.com/interviews/michael-caine-doing-something-with-nothing [accessed 8 March 2018].

One of Kamal Hassan's roles in *Appu Raja* (Singeetam Srinivasa Rao, 1989) is that of a circus clown, a dwarf. To play the dwarf, specially designed shoes were created which attached to Hassan's folded knees. For the side angle shots it was necessary to create a trench in order to conceal the actor's real legs below the knee, and holes were dug for shooting static shots. He had to practise for over two weeks to convincingly create the correct illusion at ground level that his walk looked realistic.[7]

No matter how strong the performances, a tight shot of actors of different heights is likely to look ridiculous. In the same way as we have to cheat the distance between actors for a two-shot or close-up, so the digging of trenches to stand in, or the employment of boxes to stand on, is not uncommon. Alan Ladd (five foot six) appears with Sophia Loren (five foot nine) in Jean Negulesco's *Boy on a Dolphin* (1957). A special trench was dug for Loren so that she did not tower over Ladd.[8]

Screen Actors' Motto #9:
The only truth is on the screen.

[7]Aditya Savnal, 'Here's How Kamal Hassan Became a Dwarf for Appu Raja!', Jamuura.com, blog post, 5 September 2015. Available at: http://www.jamuura.com/blog/heres-how-kamal-hassan-became-a-dwarf-for-appu-raja/ [accessed 20 May 2019].
[8]Lucy Mangan, 'A Short History of Men Standing on Boxes', *The Guardian*, 26 April 2007. Available at: https://www.theguardian.com/Columnists/Column/0,,2065602,00.html [accessed 3 March 2018].

10 FINDING THE ART OF YOU

To the actor

We have spent the previous chapters isolating the various skills of the screen actor in the hope that by focusing on specific aspects of the craft you will be able to identify in your own work areas that need to be practised and honed. The danger is, of course, that the process will have left you with the view that screen acting is just a matter of mastering a set of techniques and such nebulous qualities as talent and on-screen presence are a myth. What we hope, though, is that we leave you with an awareness of the range of techniques and protocols which need to be combined with your talent – along with no small measure of luck. By working with these exercises and reviewing your own work with others, we hope you will be able to identify the aspects of your acting that you are struggling with and which skills need further sharpening. You can then work towards the ideal – a holistic approach to the creation of a role and improved chances of success.

The authors of this book, like Doctor Frankenstein, have scoured the graveyards for pieces of the elusive competent screen actor and laid them out on the operating table. As Mary Shelley's story tells us, the most difficult body part to find is the head: the brain that controls all these disparate parts. That is you. It is your good sense, your talent and your ability to work with the camera that will ultimately bring these 'body parts' under control. It is your instinct based on preparation that will energize the electricity of your talent so that those who see you will say, 'It's alive!' This chapter is about practice in achieving this cohesion of performance.

Perhaps one of the deepest traps that awaits actors new to the screen is trying to emulate other screen actors they admire. To try to imitate

Marilyn Monroe or James Dean, Cameron Diaz or Keanu Reeves is clearly not going to progress your career. You are you and, like these actors, you need to find the specific art of you that only you have. You can learn from them but do not try to be them; they're much better at being them than you could ever be. For most novice screen actors, this temptation is irresistible but will be a passing fad, and survive only as a party trick. For some it becomes a disastrous flirtation with comparison.

The temptation to imitate works something like this. Instead of working through the text with a fresh eye, considering the backstory, listening and responding in the moment and so on, the actor thinks, 'I'll do this like Marlon Brando/Michelle Pfeiffer'. They are thinking about the end result not the creative process. This reveals a lack of faith in your own abilities and skills; you are hiding behind the persona of someone you admire. That is not what you are being paid to do. Even if you get away with it, the best reviews you can hope for will speak of your derivative style that the originals did so much better. In rehearsal this approach will get in the way of character development and the director will have a crisis on their hands. Remember (Chapter 3), you are there to do a job.

Be you

That is why we have emphasized in this book that there are a thousand different ways to deliver a line, not by mimicking the movie star but by finding within yourself that rhythm which allows the character to breathe its own life as a new and fresh interpretation that is owned purely by you, the individual actor. Avoiding interpretation through another actor's screen (or stage) performance requires a monumental feat of discipline on the part of the student actor. Sometimes in our studio work with students we have used extracts of scripts from existing films. When working with such scripts, some students will be aware of the films and the performances, whilst others will be tempted to take a sneak look at the original on DVD (against our advice) to see what somebody has done with the part they have been ask to play. What *we* were interested in was what their own talent and techniques would bring to the exercise. It was always very clear when students had been influenced (deliberately or unwittingly) by exposure to the original. Once seen, it becomes an impossible psychological battle to *un-see* it during rehearsal and performance. There is a growing appetite in movieland (born perhaps out admiration for the original, but often the result of laziness and the prospect of making an easy buck) to undertake remakes of some of the great film classics of the last one hundred years. If you are lucky enough to be offered an audition and perhaps then to be cast in such a remake, we would counsel you to avoid the temptation to model your performance on the original unless the director specifically requires it.

Consider for a moment a theatrical example. 'Remakes' are the norm in theatre, after all. How many productions of Shakespeare's *Hamlet* have there been in the last four hundred years? Undoubtedly thousands. Some of them may have even been similar, but none of them the same. Every great Hamlet, every great Ophelia, will have been different. And many, many of the thousands of interpretations across the ages will have been astounding performances. If there was only one 'perfect' way to deliver the lines, to establish the relationships, to interpret the themes, then somebody would have done it and there would be little point in doing it again. But the fact is there is no 'perfect' way and an individual's talent and performance skill can bring new insights and fresh understandings to both audiences who have seen the play before and those who are coming to it for the first time.

And so in film. What we want to see is your control of your talent and technique, creating a performance that is not imitative. Indeed, to create a performance that others will want to imitate (though, of course, we would advise against it, for they could never be you in the way that you are!).

Let us return to Doctor Frankenstein's operating table. Here are the body parts we have dissected in previous chapters:

- Adjustment of your skills from the theatre to the lens.
- The skill of keeping it real and concentrating.
- Working in the moment and responding to what is actually happening.
- Using your imagination and research to immerse yourself in the time and place of the shoot.
- Listening skills. Working with the other actors to respond truthfully to them and the situation.
- The skills needed to provide emotional coherence when a shoot is interrupted.

We have also considered:

- The technical aspects of voice and eyeline.
- Finding your mark.
- Cheating position and adjusting technique whilst maintaining belief.

You will probably have recognized that many of the exercises presented in the previous chapters cover more than the narrow topic that is being addressed. Listening is closely tied to working in the moment and accepting the circumstances of the time and place of the shoot. Working with the camera in close-up rather than a live audience at a distance is inextricably linked to finding the right vocal and physical levels, and so on. The exercises that follow here are designed to give you an opportunity to bring all these skills together in performance. They consist mainly of ideas for short films that you can create either with a tutor/workshop leader or on your own. The crucial element is to review the outcomes critically: to look for the moments where your technique could be improved and then to return to some of the other exercises in this book to sharpen these aspects of your work. Do this with your fellow actors. Try to overcome that blessed egosystem and cut through any defensiveness and feelings of hurt pride to exchange observation and advice honestly. Perhaps this is the greatest demand that you can make of yourself: to accept criticism and, even if you disagree with it, to respond to it positively – 'What is it about what I did that made others see it like that?' That is an ability truly worth having, and it is an ability that will help you bring all those disparate parts of your technique together under the control of your head and your talent. Then you will have found the art of You.

The other side of the camera

You will find that the exercises that follow invite you to not only act, but to put yourself in the shoes of other filmmaking roles, behind the camera, on a shoot (see also Exercise 7:1). Even if you have no interest in these aspects of the work (at least at this stage of your career), it can be very helpful to your understanding of the process to consider the work from the point of view of the director, camera operator, lighting designer or sound technician. It is beyond the scope of this book to go into fine detail about the pre-production elements of making a film, but here are a few things you might have to consider if you are planning to undertake a shoot with others in your group.

The first thing is that you will invariably find yourself amongst equally angst-ridden fellow Kubricks, all at the mercy of their egosystems and desperate to make the greatest film ever, regardless of the lack of time, money and facilities. For a three-minute recording, your team will spend as long as you've got, and more, discussing:

- The story.
- The character paradigms.
- Why it is that only *you* have the true vision of what this film should be?
- The storyboard (identifying key locations, moments and camera angles).
- The shot list.
- 'Can we use a supermarket trolley for a dolly shot?'
- 'If we do, who's gonna nick it?'
- 'If we do, who's gonna put it back?'
- 'What about catering if we're out there all day?'

And in all the excitement and planning, you might, like so many film crews and directors, realize:

- Oh … what about the actors?
- Should we rehearse with them? Should we let them prepare on their own?

Suddenly, the notion of the 'actor as plumber' comes back to you. The actors have seemed almost incidental to your plans. But you know from your own training and practice that they too will have been doing research, thinking about the characters, their relationships and their physical lives. They will have a notion of their backstories and their objectives and motivations. How will you accommodate their ideas in your great plan?

Yes, actors are often an afterthought. For a professional shoot these anxieties are far more complex, with vast millions of dollars at stake, and will lead to the same anxiety for all and sundry. It can affect everybody, from the clapperboard operator desperately trying to remember what shot comes next and where they put their marking chalk, to the continuity person taking copious Polaroids for fear of facing gales of laughter in the screening room as the wine bottle, with each cut, goes from full to half-empty and back again. (Even some movies made by Orson Welles are blighted by this suspension of disbelief breaker – see the fantastic disappearing/reappearing shawl in his 1968 made-for-TV movie *The Immortal Story* (1968).) Let us not forget the shaky boom operator sweating lest they commit the very public act of ruining a take by tiring for a nanosecond and allowing the extended furry sound snatcher to lower into the scene, at which point the director will shout, 'Aargh, cut! Idiot! You've ruined the best take … *ever*.' Or even worse: no one notices until it is too late.

It can be a salutary experience being on the other side of the camera, and it is one that you should embrace if the opportunity arises. Many screen actors make the transition to directing later in their careers and, for other actors at least, this is often seen as an advantage. Morgan Freeman, talking with Michael Caine on *Front Row* (BBC Radio 4, 7 April 2017), maintained that 'actors make the best directors', a view with which Caine agreed. Certainly, it is an advantage for directors and their assistants to recognize the processes and challenges their actors are facing, but it may also be true that we may be more adaptable and responsive actors if we have lived a little behind the camera and carried something of the weight of that holistic responsibility.

If, in undertaking the exercises in this chapter, you are given the task of being filmmakers as well as actors, be sure to use as many of the protocols mentioned in earlier chapters in your own studio disciplines.

- Always insist on quiet before a shoot.
- Mark the shots.
- Check camera and sound.
- Always use the command 'Action!'
- Always use the command 'Cut!'

This ritual will help engrain into everyone's consciousness the routine that ensures a shoot progresses as smoothly as possible.

For the tutor

Exactly how the following exercises are implemented will very much depend upon the technical facilities and time available to you and your trainees. If you are based in a film school or have access to substantial technical support, then they could be undertaken with professional production standards in mind. Certainly, some of these exercises would benefit from being shot from various angles and then edited, perhaps with post-production sound. We know that for many this will not be feasible, but we emphasize again that the purpose of this book is to give practice in appropriate *acting* skills. The technical wizardry will add a gloss but the underlying value and structure are based in the strength of the acting.

Students of screen acting are very keen (after initial embarrassment perhaps) to see themselves on screen and to share their presence with the world. In these times of social media prevalence, it is virtually impossible to prevent their work (of whatever value) ending up online for the world to see. Do all you can to control this desire and to at least filter what is allowed into cyberspace. Once out there it can rarely be retrieved and deleted. The serious screen actor might want to think very carefully about sharing their early attempts at film acting with the present and future population of the world. We suggest that these exercises are primarily seen as the basis of review, feedback and critical analysis so that students can revisit the exercises in other chapters to further improve aspects of their work. A young actor's career is not helped if a casting director or director has easy online access to substandard performance in a vanity project.

Again, depending on the particular environment in which you are working, you may be able to act as director of these mini-films yourself, or there may be trainee directors available to you (but see advice in Chapter 12: It's a WRAP!). You could also consider using the screen-acting trainees themselves in these filmmaking roles. This creates the need to develop the overall vision for the piece, however short it may be, and allows the actor-as-filmmaker to better understand the challenges and goals that a screen director has to achieve whilst accommodating her actors. If this approach is taken, it is usually better if the 'director' works on a film in which they won't be acting. One solution which we have used with university screen acting students is to pair the groups and assign key filmmaking roles to one group (Group A), who work with a group of actors (Group B). In this scenario Group A might consist of director, assistant director, camera operator as well as possibly a sound operator, lighting technician (if technical facilities permit) and continuity. Group B would then take on a similar set of roles for Group A. These two groups would organize themselves to shoot both their films within a given time frame. If more than one camera or angle is used, or more than one shoot is required, then the issue of editing will also have to be considered. It is a matter of adjusting the parameters of the exercises to fit the context of your working situation. But the exercises are about the acting.

Some of the exercise dialogues in previous chapters will themselves offer opportunities for a short film in which your screen actors can demonstrate their ability to meld the various aspects of screen acting that we have identified. You may also have budding screenwriters in the group and this could be their opportunity to shine. Watch out for the early tendency to over-write or to write the subtext. Again, remember that film, and even TV, is a visual medium and the text should be as sparse as possible, whilst still communicating with the audience; make the actors work.

Given the danger of using extant film scripts for practice in screen acting, the following exercises encourage the development of new material based on a range of sources. We are assuming that the creation of full-length features is not within the realm of possibility, so the suggestions here offer time- and facility-limited opportunities for the actors to practise their skills. The function of these exercises is to fuse together the techniques covered in the previous chapters. In all cases the actors should be considering the following:

- What is my backstory?
- What does my character want and what are my motivations in this scene?
- How does my character speak and move?
- What has happened to the character immediately prior to this scene?
- What am I expecting to happen in this situation?
- Am I accepting what actually does happen when I enter this situation?
- Am I allowing myself to inhabit the time and place of the shoot?

- Am I listening to the other actor/s?
- Am I showing? Or feeling?
- Am I making the other actors look good?
- Am I responding to the technical needs of the filmmaking crew?
- Am I listening?

EXERCISE 10:1 THEY'RE PLAYING OUR SONG

One source of short film material can be music lyrics. A song such as 'She's Leaving Home' by the Beatles (Lennon/McCartney, *Sergeant Pepper's Lonely Hearts Club Band*; EMI, 1967) offers a poignant situation that can be explored with very little dialogue. Remember that screen, and especially film, is primarily a visual medium. Try to tell the story of the song using as few words as possible. This can be an interesting challenge in itself. Use a mixture of long shots, two-shots and close-ups. If possible, the various scenes should be edited together, but alternatively the material can be viewed as a series of cameos:

- The girl waking, writing a note and packing her bag.
- Closing the door behind her.
- The parents discovering her absence.
- Consoling each other.
- The girl hitchhiking.
- The girl meeting her secret 'older man'.

If you decide to incorporate a soundtrack, avoid using the original song and remember that music and words may be protected by copyright law.

Variations. There are many narrative lyrics which may act as inspiration for short films and the reader will have their own ideas and predilections. Early ballads such as 'Matty Groves' (about a lord who kills a servant who is sleeping with his wife) offer non-copyright opportunities for short films as gruesome as any TV police drama.

'The Bramble Briar' also tells of a noble lady who falls in love with a servant and decides to elope. Her brothers discover the plan and murder him. Their sister demands to know the whereabouts of the servant. The brothers tell her that he disappeared when they were out in the woods and can't be found. She has a dream of her lover, dead and bloody. She finds his corpse in the briars and smothers his dead lips with kisses. After three days she cuts off his head and keeps it buried in a pot beneath a rosemary plant. One for the CSIs.

The narratives in the lyrics of Al Stewart's early albums are certainly another source of (less horrific) inspiration (*Love Chronicles* (CBS, 1969) or *Zero She Flies* (CBS, 1970)). The album *A Grand Don't Come for Free* (The Streets; Atlantic, 2004) similarly contains interesting narrative vignettes, but the reader will no doubt have their own musical library that will offer further inspiration.

Should you take inspiration from such sources, then be sure to write your own dialogue and be wary of placing material in the public domain.

EXERCISE 10:2 POETIC LICENCE

Poetry can be another source. You have a little more freedom here if you choose poems from long-departed poets and you could consider using lines of dialogue from the original works. Also, have a look at Jacques Prévert's 'Déjeuner du Matin', English translations of which can be found online. The story is briefly as follows:

- The scene takes place over breakfast where a couple are not communicating.
- Outside it is raining.
- The coffee being poured and stirred in the silence is described.
- The man lights a cigarette and blows smoke rings.
- He flicks the ash into the ashtray.
- He gets up and puts on his hat and coat.

- He leaves.
- She buries her face in her hands.
- She sobs.

This poem offers an opportunity for the portrayal of a highly intense relationship that can be played entirely without dialogue but with loads of acting! It can also be filmed in one take with close-ups, to which could be added cutaways and post-production sounds or music.

EXERCISE 10:3 HEMINGWAY'S SHOES

The story may be apocryphal but Ernest Hemingway is said to have accepted the challenge to write a novel in six words. This is what he came up with: 'For sale: baby shoes. Never worn.'

FIGURE 20 Exercise 10:3 Baby shoes for sale. Photo by Abby Timms.

Give actors and filmmakers the task of creating a time-limited film developed from this evocative advertisement. The actors in Figure 20 clearly have a tragic stimulus in mind. Are there other interpretations? You can specify the number of actors, duration, number of locations and amount of dialogue as you wish.

EXERCISE 10:4 PICK A GENRE, ANY GENRE

We have frequently stressed the need to approach text with an open mind, recognizing the fact that there are many possible interpretations of lines, situations and relationships. Some practice examples are included in earlier chapters. The following, short, original scripts are offered as additional opportunities to consider multiple interpretations. It can be an interesting experiment for groups of students to work on the same script and see if the outcomes are different. For example, as well as different approaches to subtext, the material might be variously interpreted as dramatic, soap operatic or comic. Unless the style demands it, the temptation to run the dialogue without pause should be resisted. Find the pauses. Find the moments.

Parent and Child

The Parent – or it could be a sibling with parental responsibilities – has discovered some illegal drugs in the Child's pocket. Experiment with different approaches to the relationship, different levels of concern and anger. Try switching approaches abruptly during the scene. Clearly, this scene can be played as drama. Could it be played as comedy? Where is the humour? Relationships? Reactions? Situation? Timing?

Parent	I washed your denims today.
Child	Uh-huh.
Parent	I said I washed your Levi's.
Child	Thanks.
Parent	You left a Kleenex in the pocket.
Child	Have they got fluff all over them? I was going to wear those tonight.
Parent	I found it in the pocket after I washed them. By then it was too late.
Child	It'll take ages to get it off. May as well chuck them out.

Parent	Perhaps you should empty your pockets before putting them out for me to wash.
Child	I didn't put them out. They weren't dirty.
Parent	They were on the floor with all your other dirty clothes. It's hard to tell.
Parent	Not all I found.
Child	What?
Parent	In your pockets.
Child	What do you mean?
Parent	Alex, sweetie!
Child	[Reaction, then] What are you talking about?
Parent	Haven't I always tried to steer you right?
Child	I'm going out.
Parent	Stay right where you are.
Parent	You'll kill yourself, you know.
Child	That's my choice.
Parent	Listen to yourself.
Child	I'm sixteen.
Parent	Do you think that stops me caring? I want you to be 76 one day.
Child	God. You're not the boss of me.
Parent	The law says I am.
Child	It was only a tiny bit. What did you do with it?
Parent	Flushed it.
Child	What?
Parent	Just like you're doing with your life.
Child	I'm out of here.
Parent	Where are you going?
Child	Out.
Child	I need to score.

Where is this going?

Are the couple getting together or breaking up? Is it a drama, a sitcom or a romcom?

A. You know I like you.
B. Like me?
A. A lot.
B. Me too.
A. You like you too?
B. You know what I mean.
A. Sometimes.
A. Do you mean this?
B. I think so.
A. That's not enough.
B. What would be enough?
A. Not this.
B. Everything changes.
A. Develops. Everything develops.
B. Is this what this is – a development?
A. We didn't plan it.
B. Well, I didn't.
A. What do you mean?
B. It doesn't matter.
A. It's not important.
B. It is to me.
A. What's important is this.
B. Are you sure?
A. I'm sure.
B. Sure.

EXERCISE 10:5 STREET MEET

This script offers the possibility for interpretation as a drama, sitcom or romcom. Pay particular attention to the backstories of the characters, their immediate/given circumstances and their developing objectives through the scene. The tutor may need to draw students' attention to the multiple lines of subtext that may be present (Figure 21).

(Two couples meet: SUE and ANDRE, KARL and ELLEN)

SUE (to KARL)	Hi. Long time.
KARL	Yes.
SUE	What brings you to town?
ANDRE (to SUE/KARL)	Aren't you going to introduce me?
ELLEN	I'm Ellen.
KARL (to SUE)	This your current boyfriend?
SUE (to KARL)	This is Andre. And he's my partner.
KARL	Partner. Mmm. Yes, 'boy' doesn't seem right at your age, does it Andre?
ANDRE (to SUE)	And you are?
SUE	Sue. Susan.
KARL	(to ANDRE) Your current wife?
ANDRE	My wife.
KARL	Good luck.
ELLEN (to SUE)	Should I know you?
SUE	Unlikely. I don't think you were around when we were married?
ELLEN	You're Karl's ex?
SUE	Though maybe you were around back then?
KARL	Does it matter?
ELLEN	We should make a foursome sometime.
KARL	I don't think …
SUE	I don't think so either. Leave the past in the past.
KARL (to SUE)	Anyway, you never were very experimental were you? (to ANDRE) Don't you find?
ANDRE	I …
ELLEN	See you around.
SUE	Can't wait.

FIGURE 21 Exercise 10:5 Tutor setting up 'street meet' scene. Photo by Abby Timms.

EXERCISE 10:6 NOT A WORD

We add this final suggestion as a return to where we started – to create a silent movie for a contemporary audience. Avoiding the exaggerated gestures of the early silent movies, the task is to find a contemporary non-verbal style. For inspiration only, students might like to view *The Artist* (Michel Hazanavicius, 2011) or *Blancanieves* (Pablo Berger, 2010). They may choose to add music or limited sound effects. A fun exercise in itself, the process can reinforce the understanding of the visual nature of cinema and the importance of physical communication. However, remember that we are much more sophisticated in our reading of facial clues and moods than early cinema audiences were presumed to be. The use of close-ups and other techniques may obviate the need for grand gestures and extreme expressions. Keep it real. Keep it subtle. You don't even have to keep 'quiet on the set!'

Some performances to consider

We all have our favourite films and actors and we would not have the temerity to offer definitive examples of actors bringing together their technique through the medium of their talent. Here are a couple of examples, though, where actors have been prepared to endure extraordinary discomfort in the service of their art. View the films for yourself and consider the balance of talent and technique.

Bryan Cranston, in *Breaking Bad* (Vince Gilligan, AMC, 2008–13), notes that he was emotionally tested by the scene in which his character Walt stands by whilst Jane (Krysten Ritter) chokes to death on her own vomit. He also recalls a physically arduous scene from that season in which Walt and Jesse (Aaron Paul) kidnap Saul (Bob Odenkirk) and force him to dig his own grave. 'It was like 9 degrees without the wind-chill factor, and it was really windy, and sand was kicking up and blowing in our faces,' recalls Cranston. 'I'm supposed to hold the gun out and I'm so cold that I'm shaking, and I'm like "Oh, my god . . ." That was probably the toughest scene to do.'[1]

Daniel Day-Lewis played the role of Christy Brown in *My Left Foot* (Jim Sheridan, 1989). The Brown character is a writer with cerebral palsy and a wheelchair user. During the shooting, Day-Lewis refused to leave his wheelchair between scenes in order to create a reality-bound performance that displayed symptoms associated with the condition, even to the extent of being fed by others at mealtimes. Ultimately, this approach earned him two broken ribs, sustained from his continually hunched position, but he still didn't leave the wheelchair, refusing to come out of character.[2]

Screen Actors' Motto #10:
Technique feeds my talent, my talent needs technique.

[1]Areeba Abid, 'A Method to Their Madness: Stars Who Went Way Too Far for Their Roles', Zimbio.com. Available at: www.zimbio.com/A+Method+to+Their+Madness+Stars+Who+Went+Way+Too+Far+For+Their+Roles [accessed 23 August 2018].
[2]'*My Left Foot* Trivia', IMDb.com. Available at: https://www.imdb.com/title/tt0097937/trivia [accessed 23 August 2018].

11 AUDITION PEACE

To the actor

We couldn't leave you without a few words about auditions, even though that is not the primary aim of this book. Auditions are, though, the hoop of fire through which most of you will have to dive to enter the industry, and so we offer some brief advice here based upon the techniques set out in the other chapters. There are many books and countless online sites solely devoted to preparation for auditions, so the audition 'peace' that we seek to give you here is limited: limited to our own experience and from talking to young actors, casting directors and agents.[1]

> To get an audition, you need to persuade someone to take a look at the 'product' you are 'selling,' which is yourself ... Selling is part of life in show business, as it is in any business. (Black 1990: 92)

Before you even get an audition, someone will have looked at your mugshot online, in *Spotlight* (in the UK) or *Actors Access* (in the United States). These services are generally the first port of call for casting agents and directors, and you should be in there. They will be looking at dozens of these profiles, starting with photos, seeking, in the first instance, the right 'type': does your face fit what they (or their clients) have got in mind? So, make sure your photo is neutral and shows *you*, not some characterized version of yourself. Don't play a role in the résumé photo, because you don't know what they are looking for and guessing is a lottery you're unlikely to win. There is a move at the moment in the UK, says Nicola Reynolds Casting, to cast 'real' people and you are more likely to stand out from the crowd as yourself than as some version of what you think directors want.

---

[1]We are very grateful to Judith Gay at Edward Wyman Casting, Debi Maclean of Regan Management, Nicola Reynolds Casting and the actor Tom Mumford for their help in providing the advice set out in this chapter. The information was gathered between 8 and 31 October 2018 by email and interviews.

Much of the industry is 'looks' orientated but they will still be searching for something different. The generalized Barbie and Ken lookalikes will be consigned to playing the pole dancers and pool loungers that provide the eye candy in the opening sequences of most US police dramas.

What are they looking for?

Having found some faces that 'fit', they will look at other aspects of the role. Any particular skills required? Is height important? Accent? Are there any other physical attributes they are looking for – they might even want a person who is four foot six with a broken nose. Eventually, they will whittle the possibles down to a reasonable number and bring them in to audition.

Debi Maclean of Regan Management is complimentary about the high levels of preparation that today's young actors present. You should emulate them:

> They have learned the script. They arrive thirty minutes early. They have researched the character. They look the part and they have researched the director.

This last point she regards as having the potential to make the difference between getting and not getting the part. Researching the director's work gives you a better chance of offering what they might be looking for: to indicate that you understand the style in which the project might be developed and to help you make interpretative choices with the script that are more likely to impress. Showing a genuine interest in the director's work flatters and helps you stand out. The actor Tom Mumford agrees:

> Find out as much as you can about the role, story, director and other actors involved. When an actor looks like they know their stuff, casting directors respect it.

What to wear?

This is slightly more complicated. Debi gives an example of a young actor who went up for a part set in First World War. He researched the period, shaved his facial hair appropriately and dressed in a manner that was not a 'costume' as such, but that offered a 'dapper' image he felt the part demanded. He got the job. Similarly, if you are auditioning for a role in an Agatha Christie story set in the 1930s, you might get more attention if you wear a suit or blazer and a trilby, or, for the women, a well-researched skirt or dress together with appropriate hairstyle and make-up. Help them to see you in the part. This is more difficult if you are up for a remake of *Amadeus*, but even here perhaps you could find some flamboyant accessory that helps both you and them. Tom Mumford tries to look 'neutral' for auditions, 'with a hint of the character maybe that reflects their job, life or lifestyle'. You may well find that agents and casting agents will not give advice on this; they don't want the responsibility for you not getting the job! It is part of your creative decision-making process and your interpretation of the role.

> *"Always do your research and go dressed for the part – or as close as you can get. I sometimes feel a little self-conscious on public transport if it's too specific. I did an audition for a waitress in a commercial once and practically the whole tram was full of actresses dressed as waitresses. – Ava Hunt, actor*

Suitably prepared, you arrive early. You enter the waiting room exuding confidence and there are your competitors. There will be those who confidently tell you about the work they've done and the 'big names' they've worked with, and those who will want to regale you with stories of the one that 'just got away' – 'but I had a cold that day or else I would have nailed it'. Console yourself with the knowledge that when they get into the audition room, they will be the ones who drop the coffee or bump into the furniture. Hold on to your own focus and never become one of these energy-sucking creatures. Calmly explain that you really need to concentrate but that you'd be happy to meet up and exchange notes and anecdotes after the audition.

Audition pieces?

There was a time when it was standard procedure to have rehearsed pieces prepared for audition but now actors are only rarely asked to do this. Nicola Reynolds reports that you are more likely to be sent a script in advance to learn. Do not fail to learn the lines, no matter how busy your life. Treat this as an advantage as it gives you a chance to overcome any sight-reading problems you may have. Of course, they may decide, when you are in the room, to try you with another extract from the script or even get you to read for another part: be prepared for anything. Learning the lines reflects your ability, your professionalism and your commitment.

> “*Finding some 'business' is always helpful. I was recast back into a series because I created a performance which included some very believable ballpoint pen acting that enabled me to make an interesting character clearly connected with the world in which she worked. Give it a go – the director can always say 'no' – but it's always good to offer something. – Ava Hunt, actor*

Directors may be looking for a certain interpretation but often, according to Nicola, 'we don't know what we want until we see it. It is important not to second-guess what you *think* we want.' Casting agents want to see your personality, to see the choices you have made and to gauge what you will be like as a member of the creative team. 'Be innovative,' says Tom Mumford, 'and give *your* interpretation.' In all likelihood the key roles will have been cast and they will be looking for people who can complete the jigsaw around these main characters with good humour and professionalism. Are you going to be fun to work with? And can you work with 'big names' without being overfamiliar or overawed.

> “*A Supporting Artist friend of mine was sitting next to a good-looking black actor on set and asked if he'd ever worked in South Wales. He replied that he hadn't. My friend told him he was missing a trick and went on to extol the great rates of pay appearing as an SA on* Casualty *[a hospital drama] and* Pobol Y Cwm *[a Welsh-language soap opera]. He told him he'd put a good word in for him, as he was sure he'd get a lot of work. Well, he would: it was Idris Elba! – Judith Gay, casting agent*

For a major role in a TV drama or film, the process is likely to be prolonged, with readings and recalls along the way. Be prepared to respond to what happens in the audition itself: have an idea of what you're doing but be ready to adjust.

> The first step to a better audition is to give up character and use yourself. (Michael Shurtleff)[2]

Listening (again!)

Michael Shurtleff's book *Auditions: Everything an Actor Needs to Know to Get the Part* (2009, first published 1978) remains a key source of advice for actors moving into screen acting. He stresses the importance of listening – not just to fellow actors but to all the signals you are getting from the audition task, the director or casting director. It is a fine balancing act – showing that you've got something special to offer, whilst not signalling that you are going to be a pain to work with! Many casting directors – and even directors – don't know much about acting. They have an idea of what they want but not how the actor gives it to them. Sometimes it is not until they see the results on the screen that they realize what it is they want. They may not recognize the truth they seek until you show it to them. Be alert to the signals you are getting and don't allow the cold, emotionless reading of the casting assistant to infect what you know lies in the text and subtext. Your 'acting' partner, head buried in the script, may fail to recognize that you are pausing deliberately. Your physicality, a gesture, determined eye contact, may help them to hold back whilst you take control of your delivery. If given, take direction: show you can respond.

> *"You never know what will be asked of you – be prepared for and have ideas about how you would impro around the character! – Tom Mumford, actor*

[2]'Michael Shurtleff Quotes', AZQuotes.com. Available at: https://www.azquotes.com/author/21779-Michael_Shurtleff [accessed 3 October 2018].

Preparation and appearance

When learning the lines for the audition, give plenty of thought to the possibilities of the text and the substance of the subtext. Pay attention to any stage directions so they do not catch you out: you can't 'get up' if you are already standing! Have you considered the vocal life and the physicality of the character? Have you observed people who might offer you clues as to how this character might move? Have you practised this? Can you give them what they think they want, whilst promising to be able to offer more? Hopefully, you are adept at sight-reading (see Chapter 12), so even if the script is presented to you on the day you can maintain eye contact with the other actor or the casting assistant whilst working the text.

> *"I was once so nervous in audition that I not only read the lines but the stage directions as well. – Anon*

The Wyman Agency, which works with advertising agencies, actors and walk-ons, always recommend that 'actors should look as neutral as possible and avoid tattoos, unconventional haircuts and heavy make-up. That way they are a blank canvas.' They have also noted how some auditions for this area of work are changing in the digital age and have some useful advice for actors who are asked to undertake a 'do-it-yourself' audition:

> Increasingly [. . .] actors are given a scenario and have to film themselves on a smart phone and email it in! In this day and age, my advice would probably be to get up to date with modern tech skills, so they know how to film themselves flatteringly (not the awful 'selfie' angle). I always advise making sure they have good natural light and a tidy, unobtrusive background. It's very off-putting watching an audition with piles of dirty washing or dirty crockery in the background. They may be actors, but don't need to prove it by looking like they live with Withnail![3]

[3]The film referred to is the cult movie *Withnail and I* (Bruce Robinson, 1987) about two unemployed actors who go on holiday to the countryside.

If you are placing stuff online, it needs to be technically competent. If a show tape looks amateurish, it will do you no favours, even if the acting is brilliant; it is difficult for film professionals to see beyond technical incompetence to perceive the quality of the acting. For the same reason you should refrain from placing your home-made performance movies on the web. What's out there is out there for ever and you should exert the highest levels of quality control. Tom Mumford adds that showreel pieces should be a maximum of three minutes long.

Yeah! I can do that

Are you sure? A donkey ride on the beach when you were seven does not mean you can 'horse ride'; your future career will suffer if you turn up at a shoot where the director is expecting you to thunder across hedges and fields on a stallion and you have to explain that actually you need help getting into the saddle. There are many skills that you may have that could be of interest to a casting director and will be accessible to her via *Spotlight*. Others may not be in your résumé but you should be alert to the possible requirements of the part. Perhaps the role requires you to play a parent of a baby. Have you ever held a baby? Can you do it? Look confident doing it? Do you know a baby with whom you could practise? (Please get the parents' permission and supervision! A young nephew or niece would be ideal. Do not pick one at random from the local playground.)

Other incidentally acquired 'life skills' which you may (or may not) have might include:

- cooking
- gardening
- computer skills or typing
- driving
- riding a bicycle.

Then there are more deliberately acquired skills, such as:

- horse riding
- fishing
- diving

- any sports
- driving a motorcycle/van/lorry/bus
- dancing (what types?)
- singing (hold a tune? soloist? folk? rock? opera?)
- card tricks or illusions
- DIY
- sewing/knitting
- card games.

> *"My first scene involved riding a bike, but a combination of nerves, the gradient of the hill I had to start on and the fact this was a period piece and the bike was ancient meant I couldn't get going when they called action. The guy from the props department had to give me a push. – Tom Hardman, actor*

Paul Newman's character 'Fast' Eddie Felson wouldn't be as memorable if the actor hadn't learned how to master a pool cue for *The Hustler* (Robert Rossen, 1961). Likewise, Steve McQueen's understanding of how to handle playing cards in a poker game in *The Cincinnati Kid* (Norman Jewison, 1965) was central to the character. Where would the sci-fi genre be if Linda Hamilton hadn't learned to kick and punch like a martial arts expert as Sarah Connors in *Terminator 2: Judgement Day* (James Cameron, 1991)? And what about Hilary Swank's boxing technique in *Million Dollar Baby* (Clint Eastwood, 2004)?

Think it through

Any of these skills (and hundreds more) could be part of the backstory and make-up of your character, and there are plenty of analytically critical audiences waiting to ridicule any errors you might make. There is also the contentious issue of smoking that, if you don't, you may find difficult to act convincingly. Consulting period movies or documentaries might help. Note the different way that an aristocrat holds a cigarette compared to a middle-class smoker, a factory worker, a prisoner. Note the method of lighting a cigarette in the wind, how often the cigarette is withdrawn from the mouth and what happens to the ash. Or maybe the 'ciggy' just stays in the mouth, having adhered itself to the lower lip. Since smoking became illegal in public spaces, it is hard to recall the atmosphere of a pub or bar when ashtrays and cigarettes, smoke and nicotine stains were part of the ambience. If you are playing a lifetime smoker, you don't want your eyes to water when the smoke gets in them. Similar issues apply to drug taking, and whilst some extreme 'method' actors might be tempted, we would recommend a similarly distanced form of character preparation in this case. You might like to view and pass judgement on Elliott Gould's portrayal of hard-smoking Philip Marlowe in *The Long Goodbye* (Robert Altman, 1973). In any case, we suggest that you take the advice of the smokers and ex-smokers on the set around you.

You may have seasonal allergies which need controlling or even allergies to substances like latex which may affect your ability to take a role: think it through. Again, you may have a real objection to taking a part in which you would be required to smoke/do drugs/eat meat/offend religious beliefs and so on. In a police or forensic drama, could you cope with the blood and guts (which may be real animal blood and guts)? Don't say you want the part if you are going to resist the requirements of the role.

Other skills of which you may be able to boast include accents and languages but, as with all these skills, don't lie or even exaggerate your abilities – you won't get away with it. If for some reason you are especially adept at memorizing and verbalizing medical terms, that is certainly worth mentioning – but you will spend many a sleepless night trying to commit to memory reams of medico-babble if you say you can do it and you can't. (And the same goes for 'geek-speak' in a drama driven by digital forensics.)

There is a further set of skills which you may not have (at least not in time for that audition next week) but which you may want to acquire as part of your long-term training:

- fist fighting
- wrestling
- cat fighting
- martial arts (which one/s?)

- sword fighting (broad sword/foils?)
- dagger fighting
- gun fighting (what types of firearms?)
- knife fighting.

You should take any opportunity to undertake skills workshops in multiple areas – if you are happy to accept roles that involve such skills. Training to be a screen actor does not stop when you get your first role. There will always be 'lean times' and, even if you are waiting tables until the next opportunity, it will be essential to keep developing both your skill set and your physical control. For your physical and mental health, you could consider such workshops as

- dance
- martial arts
- meditation
- running
- yoga.

Analyse your weaknesses on screen and identify where your training needs to take you next. We must work on ourselves, as this is the basis of the characters we are trying to create.

A final word or warning. If you say you have a skill and you haven't, you will cost the production company time and money. You will never be trusted again.

Hey! You got the part

So let's just remind ourselves of the next part of the process. Maybe it's 'just' a commercial, but even so you need to be totally professional, or maybe you have one line as a taxi driver or the central role of an international diamond smuggler. You may be an alien encrusted with latex or a zombie dripping with fake (you hope) blood. The degree of preparation will vary but will be based on the ideas suggested in this book. Yes, it's that darned backstory, together with the physical and emotional life, plus your motivations, objectives and superobjective. If you are a zombie, then physicality will be important, together with the sole objective of eating the brains of living people whilst not getting your head severed. If you're that taxi driver, then knowing your way around the car, the taxi business and making sure you get paid will be part of the *character*, whilst the *actor* is coping with the demands of working with back projection.

Oh, you didn't get the part

Be ready. This will happen. A lot. And you are going to need to have resilience and the ability to get over it. Worse still if your best friend gets the part. Acting is a career that brings people close together but is also riddled with insecurities and jealousies. Rejection can feel personal when it is not. Let it go. Take care of your mental health. Consider meditation or yoga to help you deal with disappointment and objectively go over what you did or didn't do right. If you hire someone to remodel your house, you are not condemning those who didn't get the job – you've just taken on the person you feel will give you what you want. Our best advice is to look dispassionately at why you didn't get the part (and maybe why your best mate did). The answer is probably that the director or casting director simply had a concept in their head that you didn't fit. You didn't get the part but hopefully you did enough, showed enough talent/skill/integrity/professionalism to be remembered. They may have seen several or even dozens of auditionees and all those 'rejected' will be feeling the disappointment and grievance. 'You know you could have done it'? Then pick yourself up and walk tall into the next opportunity.

> *"Rejection is the worst part of being an actor and dealing with it is so important. Every actor, no matter at what level, has to deal with rejection. Analyse your audition briefly, think about how you could improve and what you did well and then move on. Don't beat yourself up – if you didn't get the job, you just weren't right for the role this time; one day you will be. Overthinking why you didn't get a part can be really detrimental for your state of mind. – Tom Mumford, actor*

Be ready to discover that friendships, and even relationships, can fail to survive the harshness of this business. 'Audition *peace*'? Sorry, we lied about that.

It can be hard to contain your excitement at getting an audition, but think carefully before enthusiastically telling friends and family. If you tell everybody you know, and you get the job, then that is terrific, but if you tell everybody and you don't get the job, then you will spend days going over the same story of rejection again and again to friends, family and neighbours. For the sake of your sanity it might be best to save your excitement for the day you can burst into the diner, throw your McDonald's cap into the fryer and declare, 'I got the part!'

Final thoughts

Here are a few final thoughts from the casting directors who have offered much of the advice in this chapter:

- The very fact that you are in the room means you have succeeded; you have been chosen from dozens. They already like you. Now, show the best version of you.
- Be ready for the unexpected. During the audition the casting assistant may want to take extreme close-up stills or video to show to the director. Keep acting. Remember that the camera picks up everything, so you need to be fully committed to the character all the time; that is what the camera and the director will see.
- If someone enters the room or the director's phone goes off, carry on and don't lose your concentration. Your professionalism in carrying on will impress. Stop only when they say 'stop' – just as you wait for 'Cut!' on a shoot.
- When you are working, remember to put money aside to pay your tax!
- Be ready for the reality of this life. It's tough. It's heartbreaking at times.
- Don't turn down auditions. You have a view of yourself and what parts you could play. Others may see you differently. Get away from the idea that there are only certain parts you are 'right' for.

Even if you are correct, you will at least gain audition experience. You may even get the part.

- Although it may not be advisable long term to take Supporting Artist ('extra') work, don't ignore the fact that key roles may have few or no lines. The shadowy villain in the bushes may have a high profile in the film and key narrative importance but few or no lines. Counting lines is what you did when acting in the school play and has no place in your professional life. The impact of your performance is what is important. You don't need lines to be crucial.
- Enjoy the audition. If you enjoy doing it, they will enjoy watching you.

To the tutor

By the time your protégées are actively seeking work, they will probably have left your sphere of influence. Some will be constantly contacting agents and casting directors, watching out for open castings and networking with fellow actors for rumours of opportunities coming up. In between they will be honing their skills, practising sight-reading, watching quality performances on screen and trying to survive financially. Others will have maybe created a website, sent out a few CVs or résumés and are now content to watch daytime telly whilst waiting for Spielberg to call. Oh, and trying to survive financially.

It may be, though, that they come to you for advice on auditions and here we offer a few exercises that may help them develop the skills and flexibility in audition situations.

EXERCISE 11:1 I'M ON THE PHONE

This exercise offer actors the chance to demonstrate a range of vocal nuance as well as their ability to internalize feelings which the camera can, in Kazan's phrase, 'penetrate'. The recorded outcome could form the basis of an online presence or be submitted as an audition tape if appropriate.

Record against a neutral background with good lighting on the face. The character is on the phone and we only hear his or her side of the conversation. There is a subtext to the 'conversation' – what is being said may be at odds with the feelings of the character. Our only clue to what the person on the other end of the line is saying is the actor's reactions. Inspiration may be drawn from the previously mentioned performance by Tom Hardy in *Locke*. The actor's task is to make us believe the totality of the situation, from backstory to dealing with the moment-to-moment reality of the call. For example:

'We've already discussed this … Yes, but … That's not what we agreed … You said, when we were … That's not how I remember it … So where do we go from here? … I don't think that would work … Because … No, because … You are not listening to me … You were the one who said we needed to communi … I'm not angry. Am I raising my voice …? I'm not angry … I'm not … Okay, you go first. Tell me what you want to happen … I'm listening … No, I'm listening, I am. [Long pause. Is the character listening? Or holding the phone away from their ear in boredom? Something else?] Mmm … Mmm … Yeah … Okay … You said it … Mmm … Have you finished? … No, I get it. I'll do that … No, I will … I will. I'll call you … Soon. Tomorrow. Tomorrow, okay? Okay.'

To successfully carry out this exercise the actor needs to know both sides of the conversation.

FIGURE 22 Exercise 11:1 I'm on the phone. Photo by Abby Timms.

Variation. In this version there is someone else in the room (Figure 22). As well as dealing with the conversation, the actor has to cope with this other presence. Are they sharing their annoyance with this person? Trying to hide something from them? Trying to convince them that what they are saying on the phone is true? The web of backstory, relationships and objectives can be as impressively complex as desired.

EXERCISE 11:2 NEXT!

A fun group exercise that nonetheless will help the student actors prepare for audition situations. Recording is not required but be ready to discuss what might be learned from it.

Use a page or two of script or screenplay involving one or two 'auditionees'. Allow them to have sight of the material beforehand or not, as you wish. The rest of the group is going to audition them and require different interpretations – more menacing, more humour, get angrier, more insecure, less knowing, more brash etc. It doesn't matter if the instructions make sense of the screenplay in question; the challenge (and the fun) is trying to respond to the requirements of the auditioners, however ridiculous. In Figure 23 we show this exercise undertaken with the additional pressure of having the casting agent's assistant film the actor's every move as a record for the director. After this exercise they should be ready for anything in an actual audition!

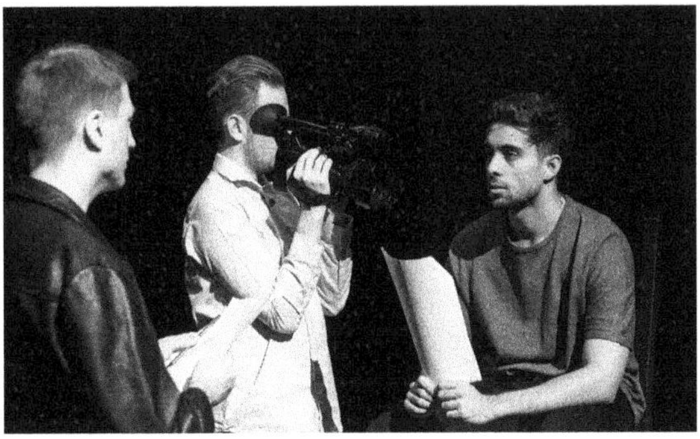

FIGURE 23 Exercise 11:2 Next! Setting up a mock audition. Photo by Abby Timms.

EXERCISE 11:3 DON'T PHONE IT IN

As mentioned earlier in the chapter, actors often find themselves reading for a part with someone who is not an actor and can't even read with any level of enthusiasm or interpretation. This exercise will help prepare the actor for these situations.

Either give the actor time to prepare by studying or even learning the script extract beforehand or allow a few minutes for them to scan through the script and make decisions about the character, their emotional and mental state.

Then ask them to read for the part with a fellow member of the group, who is instructed to read it as if they have no acting ability. They can pause oddly, trip over words and give a reading that is emotionally dead. The challenge for our auditionee is to maintain her level of preparation, to read with the emotional colour, textual insight and subtextual awareness that she had prepared – despite the total lack of any response from the coffee-sipping associate. Just because you are getting nothing back, don't 'phone in' your performance. Make a conscious effort to connect with and engage the reader, through appropriate gesture, intensity and eye contact. When you have been working with a group of actors, bouncing off each other emotionally, finding rapport and relationship at every turn, to work with an automaton is tough. But it may happen, so it's good to sharpen the skills that will allow you to surf on the top of such a wave of apparent indifference.

EXERCISE 11:4 WHY?

It is easy to overlook stage directions when preparing a reading and even more so when sight-reading a piece for the first time. Here is a short dialogue for actors to try and which depends heavily on being aware of the stage directions:

1 A. What did you do that for?
2 A. What did you do that for?
3 B. I did it.
4 A. Why?
5 B. I did.
6 A. (about to speak)
7 B. It.
8 A. I want to kn—
9 B. Why. Why?
10 A. Why?
11 B. Why do you want to know why?
12 A. It affects me too, you know.
13 B. (about to speak)
14 A. When you do that. Things like that.
15 B. Sorry.
16 A. Why?
17 B. (irritated) What?
18 A. Why are you sorry?
19 B. I can't remember.
20 A. Talk to me! (A slaps B)
21 B. Why did you do that?
22 A. I did it. I did.

By now all your students will recognize that there are many ways of playing this scene. But there are decisions that need to be made, whatever the situation is deemed to be:

Opening of scene. What is it that B has done?
Line 1 is repeated. Why? What is B's reaction?
Line 6 What is A about to say?
Line 8 What was A going to say?
Line 13 What was B going to say?
Line 17 Why is B irritated. What is A's reaction?
Line 20 What is the impetus for the slap? Where does it 'come from'? What is B's reaction?

All this is, of course, part of the usual concerns with text and subtext, motivations and objectives. Crucially, though, if the actor has only picked up on their lines, they will miss these key moments which are part of their character's story. Record and review this scene with different pairs of actors.

Screen performances to consider

You might find it useful to review some auditions by now-famous actors. Start with https://www.youtube.com/watch?v=ju5_79YOlqM.[4] Would you have given them the job? Why?

Screen Actors' Motto #11:
Give them what they want – and then some.

[4]Accessed 3 December 2018.

12 IT'S A WRAP!

I'll always be around because I'm a skilled professional actor. Whether or not I've any talent is beside the point.

MICHAEL CAINE[1]

To the actor

As we explored in Chapter 10, talent is a real thing but it is fed and nurtured by a professional development of your skills and techniques. This is not always clear-cut: perhaps you know actors who work hard, dedicate themselves to their art and yet don't seem to get the breaks. Then there are those earning megabucks in blockbuster films and TV series for whom you have no respect at all. Maybe you watch them and think 'Yeah, I've seen him/her play this role in every performance s/he's given!' Some do seem to make a living out of being 'personality actors' where it is their own persona that drives every similar characterization. And yet there are some highly watchable films and enjoyable performances that use these actors. And then there are the true 'character actors' who can employ a variety of skills and surprise you with their performance range.

What we hope we have done in this book is to give you some ways to take the process of screen acting apart, examine and polish each component and then reassemble them in order to have the best chance of success. Success is never guaranteed and to survive you need to love the art form of acting rather than be in love with fame and fortune. Aim to be an artist, not a celebrity. In this chapter we will reiterate some of the ideas we have put forward earlier in the book, whilst adding in a few thoughts that may have been bypassed on the way.

---

[1]Neil Norman, 'Michael Caine: Aged 75 and in it for the Money', *Daily Express*, 12 March 2008. Available at: https://www.express.co.uk/expressyourself/37773/ [accessed 3 October 2018].

"Once I was cast in a television commercial playing a crazy street preacher, trying to get converts for a car dealership. It was only supposed to be a short thirty-second spot, so I figured it would probably take less than an hour to complete and would require maybe five or six takes at most and I'd have plenty of time to get to my part in a Broadway show that night. I learned something that day: don't panic or get dejected when they do multiple takes; you don't know why they're doing it. After about the tenth take, I felt like a complete failure. I kept apologizing, thinking I was delivering a bad performance. After the twentieth take and the thirtieth take, I was convinced of this. I simply lost count after the fortieth take. The shoot lasted over ten hours: filming takes a long time.

I later found out that the director had been hired to shoot several ads, and she was shooting each ad in a different cinematic style. Mine was being shot in cinéma-vérité *style (as though someone who just happened to be passing by the car dealership had seen me outside preaching and quickly decided to take out their camera and start filming it). It veered in and out of close-ups and long shots, went in and out of focus, in and out of frame, and caught the noise and activity of all the traffic passing by the car dealership outside that day. It turned out to be a very clever and popular ad. I got to my Broadway show later for my call, but thankfully with half an hour to spare before the curtain went up. – Mark Gowers, actor*

Our approach to screen acting is based on backstory (Chapter 2) and listening (Chapter 7). In terms of your screen acting ability, all will stem from these. The technical aspects of working on a shoot are covered in Chapters 3 and 9. The exercises have been designed to give you confidence and competence in both the acting and technical protocols.

At times in the exercises we have indicated that you could play around with different genres, but perhaps we should include a little more. (A list of key film and TV genres is included in the Glossary section.)

Genres

We have avoided talking too much about different film and TV genres because each deserves a book of its own. For those wanting to consider in depth differing comedy acting styles, for example, we would recommend Jeremiah Comey's *The Art of Film Acting* (2002; see Recommended Further Reading). When watching comedy, get your research brain engaged – *why* it is (or is supposed to be) funny. The witty lines? The out-and-out jokes? The absurd situations? The exaggerated characters? The vocal or physical life of the characters? Watch out for the punchlines. The timing. Do some lines require being undercut or even 'thrown away'? If auditioning for a comedy part, the basic rule is to understand *why* it is funny. If shooting before a live audience, you will have the live response and will need to pause for laughs and 'ride' the laughter as in theatre. There will also be the issue of retakes, new lines being thrown at you by maybe a whole panel of writers and then having to be funny over and over again as the audience hears the joke for the sixth time. If a 'laughter track' is being used, then you have no control at all, but fortunately this is increasingly rare. If there is no audience (and this applies especially to film comedy), you will be acting in complete silence and, when you're trying to be funny, that is scary.

> *"Very often you will not get a script in advance for a soap – you won't even be able to take it with you into the toilets in case you take a photograph of it and mail it to the newspapers. Get there at least forty-five minutes early and then spend the time doing your homework, analysing the character, developing your performance and learning the script. What is important is not necessarily how you are delivering your lines but you're listening and reacting and responding to what the other character is saying. This is where the director gets to see your acting. So don't look down at the script. – Ava Hunt, actor*

Other genres present their own challenges. In previous chapters we have mentioned the problem of delivering complicated language at high speed in medical and other procedural series. In a daily televised 'soap' you may have the challenge of rehearsing (or not), shooting all day and then learning your lines for the next day when you get home. Not good for your social life and far from glamorous. Sci-fi movies and series may entail hours in full body make-up and the consequent limitations on eating, drinking and bodily functions, and all without even recognition or fame – 'did you see me in *Dr Who*? I was scaly cyberlizard number six who fell into the Time Well … They dubbed my scream.' Mmm.

> *"A new extra on set, hearing a rather flamboyant director shouting 'General atmos! General atmos!', turned to me and whispered, 'Which one is General Atmos?' – Judith Gay, casting agent*

Working with the director

In matters of genre and style you will have to be guided by the director, whilst being sure to offer something useful in return. In comedy you will need the benefit of the director's overview to reassure you that what you are doing is 'right' and 'funny' despite the deafening silence in the studio. At times, having sorted out your own pathway through the whole script, you may sometimes want to ever so gently challenge what the director asks you to do. Don't push it. She does have the last word.

Just like actors, directors come in all shapes, sizes and temperaments. Some, as we have seen, have been actors themselves and they may work very differently from those whose current butterfly status has emerged from the caterpillar state of camera operator and who have no concept of how an actors prepares and produces a performance. As well as all the artistic concerns of the acting, the lighting, the sound, the camera angles and filters, he will also have the backers and the agents and legal department to negotiate with. It is just possible that he might get a little stressed. As the daylight fades and the crew is about to go into unaffordable overtime and he still can't quite get the performance he needs from *you*, there may be harsh tones used, and even harsher language. There shouldn't be, but it might happen.

A director sympathetic to the working processes of the actor might, for example, understand the need to modulate her tone of voice to guide the actor: it is a love scene. The man is going away to war and may not return. He sits with his wife on a bench in the park where they first met. The mood is sombre. Both characters are deeply bound up in their thoughts: he dwelling on what he has to say, she concerned that he may never return. The camera is rolling, sound is rolling. 'ACTION!!!' screams the panicking director – and the mood is lost. How much better it would be to almost whisper the shooting instructions and ease the actors into their dilemma and facilitate a moving performance.

The personal, the private and other intimate stuff

In Chapter 1 we discussed the key differences and approaches between stage and screen acting. There is an additional difference that we want to bring up here. In stage acting, even if you know little about your fellow actors on day one, by the time you get to the dress rehearsal you will be working together as a team and, most probably, be friends with a mutual respect for each other's talents and a tolerance for each other's foibles. Turning up for a day's shoot, or even when involved in a more substantial role over a period of weeks, is going to be different. You will feel the pressure each day to prove yourself, and this can incite unnatural acting and a lack of respect for your fellows. Try to be yourself (whatever that is) off the set so that if you have to curse, abuse, embrace, kiss or trick a fellow actor in their role on the set, you not only impress with your professionalism but you also have the safety zone of your real identity to return to after 'Cut!' is called. Your character may be an awful SOB but you will have had to find an empathy with her without compromise. You may have to momentarily hate your friends (or love your enemies) in the shoot, and the separation of personal and professional is going to be important. Don't take it personally – neither the insult nor the loving kiss.

> *"I wish I hadn't drunk so much fizzy pop when I was nervous on my first day on set. The trapped wind escaping was like a bomb going off. Everyone stopped filming and gave me a round of applause. – Maria Palios-Potts, actor*

And a few words about screen intimacy. Working as a professional, such requirements will be specifically mentioned in your contract. Read it carefully. We recommend that you be unionized and only work on union contracts. That being said, whether you accept such roles will be up to you. Refusing certain aspects of what the director wants to shoot will not necessarily mean you won't get the part (though, in all honesty, it is less likely), but if they want you in their film badly enough, they may employ a body double for certain shots.

It you are undertaking such roles, you should find that access to the set will be restricted to essential operatives only – director, camera and sound – and the AD standing by with a robe. But there will be your fellow actor or actors. We recommend that, even if rehearsal is limited, you take the time to discuss with them what is acceptable and what is not. Aspects of the kiss, the caress, the simulated lovemaking need the same attention and emotional preparation (perhaps more) as any other requirements of the part. Personal and oral hygiene will be important (Michael Caine always carries a breath-freshening spray for use on himself *and* his acting partner). Probably one of the greatest challenges will be to control your nervous giggles.

Don't forget it's acting. Abuse of the situations is abuse. It's not real and so don't assume it is. We draw your attention to the Equity UK guidelines set out at the end of the Introduction. Respect your fellow professionals and don't get a reputation that might ruin your career.

Health

A great piece of advice from Nicola Reynolds is to take care of your health – mental and physical. Have a life outside work and develop strategies to deal with the inevitable rejection – 'part of the job is not getting the job', she says. There will be days when you are not feeling your best. Maybe you've got a sports injury or your rheumatism is flaring up or your hormones are in overdrive. In movies about movies, actors frequently have tantrums and retire to their trailers, but in real life the shooting schedule (or the audition schedule, for that matter) is sacrosanct; almost nothing will allow it to be changed. You've been around your body for all your life and you know what trouble it can cause, so be prepared. If you are ill, you just have to work through it and you shouldn't expect much sympathy from the director and his team; they've got everything else to think about. Above all, avoid self-inflicted wounds: turn up with a hangover or smelling of booze and the job is likely to be your last. Directors know each other. They network, and when they are looking for ways to reduce the casting pool from fifty down to one, actors' unreliability or unprofessionalism gives them an easy way to whittle down the list of possibles.

Your body is your artist's canvas

So certainly look after your health, but beware of stereotyping your body shape. Real life is full of all shapes and sizes, and the whole range should be reflected in film. Yes, we know that isn't always true and that some casting directors tend to favour certain 'looks', but things are changing and there is a move to more diversity of appearance and increasingly the non-typical is what the directors want to find.

Be mindful of your appearance. Painters have their canvas, sculptors their marble and musicians their instruments. Actors have only their bodies as their medium. It may already be too late, but be careful what you put on this canvas: don't scribble on it. As mentioned in Chapter 11, if you are already famous, the production company may be willing to fork out a lot of money to hide that neck tattoo but, to be honest, if you are auditioning for a part in a Jane Austen adaptation, then it is going to be easier for them to employ someone who has not got a curly snake slithering up their cheekbone or 'love' and 'hate' tattooed on their knuckles. You may get the part of the biker or the streetwalker (now who's being stereotypical!), but you are unlikely to get the part of the banker or the schoolteacher. If you must have tattoos, do not let them stray below the wrists or above the neck. The same considerations apply to piercings because, even if removed, the telltale holes might be seen in close-up HD. Generally, we would advise thinking very carefully about any body transformation: unnaturally white teeth or inflated botoxed lips may restrict the range of roles for which you might be considered. And whatever you do, do not change your hairstyle or get a tan (real or fake) in the middle of a shoot!

> *"I was chomping at the bit when I got my first professional screen part. We shot the first half of the scene in an old Dublin theatre. Then we wrapped, with a call for two weeks later to return*

and finish the scene. I took a few days away and, somewhere, decided to get a haircut. A very tight haircut. I'd totally forgotten about finishing the scene back in the theatre. When I arrived professionally on time after my break, I was on set all of five minutes before the director saw my fashion sense on display and uttered two words: you're fired! They had to shoot with a stand-in that looked nothing like me. – Paul Conway, actor

Our last word of warning is about social media. As savvy young actors, you will know the dangers of social media posts, including tweets, blogs and photographs. They are probably out there in the ether for ever. The image you want to project to your friends now may be very different from the image you want to portray as a serious film actor in the future. Opinions you may have in a self-confident and swaggering youth may seem somewhat embarrassing when republished by the tabloids when you are famous (we hope).

When will I be famous?

Be honest with yourself. Thousands of actors emerge from drama schools all over the world each year. Statistically, very few will find any security, let alone fame, in the business. The majority of those who get work get it because they love the art form, not themselves. They relish the creation of performance, with all its challenges and angst. We hope that the talent you have, together with the techniques we have offered in these chapters, will help you find the success you crave. And that will also take luck. Do people make their own luck? Yes: but it is carved out of hard work and perseverance.

Even if you successfully enter this weird and wild world of screen performance, there will be challenges ahead for which we cannot prepare you. The digital world is affecting screen performance as much as any other aspect of our lives. Increasingly, the worlds of gaming and acting seem to be merging. A colleague who worked in motion capture once remarked to me that 'soon we won't need actors at all'. I don't think he was right because motion capture only makes sense if it successfully captures the motion of real human beings. And it doesn't capture psychology and motivation. But who can tell where AI will take us in the next years and what might be the effect of AI and CGI on acting? Will the avatars get more human or will actors be required to perform more like avatars? How will we – that is *you* – keep on top of an industry where technologies and platforms are changing so fast? Will fashions in acting change and, yes, will there be actors? Until the sad day comes when actors have been replaced by CG holograms, there will always be a need for preparation, teamwork, organization, good communication and mutual respect. We hope that these exercises and the accompanying information will help you be ready for 'Action!'

To the tutor – but to actors too!

The importance of reading

Your students won't thank you for it, but there is a real need to read:

> Don't say you don't have enough time. You have exactly the same number of hours per day that were given to Helen Keller, Pasteur, Michelangelo, Mother Teresa, Leonardo da Vinci, Thomas Jefferson, and Albert Einstein. (Brown 2007: 74)

We don't – can't – know everything, and the young actor will inevitably come up against some aspect of history or current affairs or references to people or facts and objects about which they know little or nothing and yet which appear to be important to their character. The best way to prepare themselves for this is to read widely, and to be prepared to research particular matters that are pertinent to the project they are auditioning for or are performing in. They shouldn't go for a part in the latest conspiracy movie about 'who shot Kennedy' without knowing who Kennedy was.

We know they probably hate reading but, as an actor, their job is to reflect and interpret some aspect of the world as it is/was/will be. If their only knowledge of the world comes from celebrity Twitter feeds and what they've seen other actors do, their performance range will be limited and derivative. They need to read as part of research because:

- They need to understand their character's world view.
- They will be able to engage in discussion with the director and fellow actors.
- They need to develop appropriate backstories, physicality and vocal lives for their characters.
- They must be able to respond appropriately to situations and text. And listening and responding are fundamental.
- They will need to be able to read fluently, confidently and with understanding in auditions where they might be presented with a script they've not seen beforehand.

Sight reading (acting with script in hand) and 'cold reading' (acting using a previously unseen text in hand) are skills they will need. There will be occasions when they will have no idea about the project or the script, either because of poor organization or commercial secrecy.

EXERCISE 12:1 READING BETWEEN THE LINES

Students can practise sight reading and cold reading with fellow actors using any scripts available, though it is probably more useful to choose plays or screenplays that they don't know and haven't seen performed. Play scripts are easily accessed from a library or bookshop and it is also possible to access screenplays and TV scripts online, which have the advantage of showing exactly how a film or TV script looks on the page. Here are some examples to get them started (along with the screenwriters' names):

- *On Golden Pond* – Ernest Thompson
- *Bonnie and Clyde* – Calder Willingham and Buck Henry
- *Bridget Jones's Diary* – Helen Fielding
- *Saturday Night and Sunday Morning* – Alan Sillitoe
- *Thelma and Louise* – Callie Khouri

The aim of the exercise is to practise sight reading and to develop the intuition for character, situation and relationships that may be required in an audition. Ask the actors to share ideas about these aspects of the script and the assumptions they made, and then allow re-reading. Invite them afterwards to view the actual films or film versions of the plays to understand how their interpretations were different. And maybe they were better!

EXERCISE 12:2 COLD READING THE NEWS

This exercise can be undertaken at home or in a workshop situation. The actor is required to try to read a section from an unseen newspaper article whilst maintaining eye contact with a fixed point (the camera, the director, the casting director, the clock on the wall). It's something that a good public speaker will do when working from notes, and it is an invaluable skill in audition situations (Figure 24). Ask them to read the piece 'straight' and then with a character-based intention underlying the text – appreciation, mockery, irony, disdain, enthusiasm.

FIGURE 24 Exercise 12:2 Cold reading. Photo by Abby Timms.

EXERCISE 12:3 SPEAK *AND* ACT?

The actors could undertake these sight or cold readings 'on location', where they can absorb how ambient sounds affect their vocal impulses and tones. As far as is possible with script in hand, they can try carrying out an activity to augment the script – rolling a cigarette, drinking a coffee, turning a coin between the fingers – whatever seems appropriate. If the actor is able to involve some ideas for such minor physicality into a script-in-hand audition, it will impress. Nor should they overlook the possibilities for eye contact, subtle emotional reaction and awareness of the performance of others. In an audition, the director will be looking for signs that not only can the actor find her character but that she can show awareness of others, listen and respond appropriately. No doubt the process will be filmed and all these clues as to the actor's ability will be noted. You could undertake part of this exercise in a studio situation and analyse the audition process with them.

EXERCISE 12:4 I WASN'T EXPECTING THAT!

This exercise will help prepare actors to adjust their backstory and their objective or superobjective when working with material they have not had the opportunity to study beforehand. Its inspiration is an early scene from *Butch Cassidy and the Sundance Kid* (George Roy Hill, 1969) where Sundance (Robert Redford) appears to be about to rape Etta Place (Katharine Ross) at gunpoint – 'keep goin' lady': a very disturbing introduction to a character we were expecting to be one of our heroes. The uncomfortable tension is released when it turns out that the whole set-up is role-play – 'You know what I wish? That once you'd get here on time!' says Etta. Imagine an actor reading that screenplay for the first time and starting to construct a backstory, a psychology and a motivation based solely on the text and stage directions. Then you turn the page and discover that it is all part of their foreplay.

The student actors can go back to some improv for this one. Ask them to prepare a piece in twos or threes on a theme of your or their choosing – a love triangle, a heist, an exploration of an alien planet, an interrogation, a family celebration. Give them time to prepare a basic backstory, motivations and objectives. Stop the improv at what appears to be a promising point (or when it is in danger of running out of steam) and invite the group watching to throw in a new piece of information which the improvisers have to cope with and which may involve immediately rethinking their backstory and their actions: the lovers are brother and sister; no one in the gang knows how to drive the getaway car; the alien planet turns out to be prehistoric Earth; someone lets slip that the child is adopted …

It is an exercise in quick thinking and taking on board new information without jettisoning what has already been established. Somehow make it work!

If you are successful in forging a career – a life – as a screen actor, then there is perhaps one other thing to remember. It should be hard work – but it should be fun.

"I was on my first shoot as a background artist, working on Scottish Mussel *[Talulah Riley, 2015], and it was quite a steep learning curve; but the highlight was finding myself dancing the Gay Gordons with an otter-wrangler called Daphne! – Sophie Houston, actor*

Screen performances to consider?

This time we leave it to you. Watch anything and everything and expand your knowledge of all forms of screen acting. But watch the screen critically. What can you learn and what can you learn to avoid? What would be your best ten films of all time and why?[2]

Screen Actors' Motto #12:
Luck is made of talent, hard work and perseverance.

FIGURE 25 Photo by Paul Conway.

[2]If you find that they are all romcoms, or all sci-fi movies, or all action movies, start again!

GLOSSARY

Technical screen shooting terms

Action Called out by the director as a signal for the actors to begin.

AD Assistant director. If you have questions about the process, it will probably be to her that you enquire.

Angle The relation of the recording camera to the action being played.

Back Projection Now largely superseded by CGI, back projection is filmed separately and then reshot with the actors playing their parts and interacting with the pre-filmed images. An example would be *Jason and the Argonauts* (Chaffey, 1963) and can frequently be seen in driving sequences, where the actors drive a static car in the studio whilst the filmed background gives the illusion of movement.

Boom Mic The microphone, usually with a fur baffle covering it, which is suspended by the boom operator above the actors to record the sound.

CGI (Computer Generated Imagery) In film and TV, CGI is the use of computer graphics to create the visual environment in which the action takes place and even the characters or creatures with whom the performer may be interacting. (*See also* Green Screen.)

Cheating The technical adjustments that are made to the blocking in relation to the camera so that the recorded action looks natural when played back. See Chapter 9.

Clapperboard This board has a mechanism which, once the identifiers of the take have been announced by the operator (name of project, episode number, scene number, take number), can be 'clapped', producing a short, sharp sound. This enables the editor to synchronize sound and visual recordings. Traditionally, these are blackboards marked with chalk, though white boards and markers are also in use. Digital clapperboards are now increasingly common.

Close Up (CU) The camera is focused tightly on the actor's face.

Continuity Generally ensuring that the costume, hair and make-up remain consistent from take to take. Also that props are historically correct and are positioned properly, that bottles and cups face the same way, that consumables are reset accurately between takes. For actors it will mean finding consistency in emotions, movements and gestures in each take.

Cut Called by the director at the end of the scene. Sound and camera recording will be stopped at this point. Actors should not stop the scene themselves, even if they think something has gone wrong.

Cutaway An inserted visual placed by the director and editor during the action. For example, a glimpse of something happening outside the window whilst the characters are talking, or a shot of another character's reaction.

Diegetic Sound Sound that is supposedly happening in the scene – for example, music in a club or from a radio. This is different from the film score, which is external to the action and added to set the mood or increase tension. Both will usually be added post-production.

Dolly The equipment on which a camera is mounted to run on the tracks (*see* Tracking). Hence **dolly camera** and **dolly shot**.

Eyeline Where an actor's character is supposed to be looking, even if the person or object has to be imagined. See Chapter 9.

Extras *See* Supporting Artists.

Extreme Close-Up (XCU) Even tighter than a close-up. The camera will be focusing on (for example) just your eyes or the sweat on your brow.

Finding Your Mark Moving to the correct position during the action. If sitting on a chair, you will either need to leave the chair on its mark or move it there when you sit in the agreed rehearsed position.

Go Again If the director wishes to 'go again', he wants to reshoot the same scene from the same angle – i.e. he or she wants to go for another take.

Green Screen In Green Screen the actor performs the action in front of a green screen which is replaced technologically by an image that creates the illusion of the completed environment. It is important not to wear the same green in your costume as that part of your anatomy would disappear!

In the Can The scene is finished with, and the director is happy with what has been recorded.

Long Shot (LS) A shot taken from a distance and incorporating the actors and their surroundings.

Looping This is the filmmaking term for dubbing, mixing or re-recording in post-production. It is the process by which new vocal recordings are mixed with the original material for technical or artistic reasons.

Mark It The director is ready to record. It is an instruction to the clapperboard operator to step forward, place the clapperboard in view of the camera, announce the take and 'clap' the board.

Medium Shot (MS) A camera shot which takes in the actors but largely excludes their surroundings.

Noddies Mainly used in news recording, but you may hear the term. When only one camera and operator is available, the key person or interviewee is recorded responding to questions and then the same camera is reversed to record a generic and general variety of reactions from the interviewer to what was said. These are edited together to make it look as if the interviewer has reacted in real time to what was said by the interviewee. It also offers opportunities for the editor to cut out sections of the interview.

OOV (Out of View) If you see this direction in a screenplay, it means that the actor's lines that follow are being spoken from outside the filmed action.

For example, one person might be having a conversation with another in an adjoining room. This will affect voice tone and levels. See Chapter 9.

OS (Over the Shoulder) The camera is placed behind and to the side of one of the actors so that it can catch the interaction as if it were the person being talked to.

Panning The camera follows the action without cutting from angle to angle, or takes in a wide view – a panorama – of the surroundings. The lateral movement of the camera, normally mounted on a tripod, to follow the action or to find another subject to frame.

Pick Up If a shot has to be abandoned before it is 'in the can', the director may instruct the crew to 'pick up' in the morning (or whenever).

Pitch Trying to sell an idea to a production company.

Post-Production What happens after the shoot. Even after the editing, there will be sound, music and special effects to add.

POV (Point of View) The camera is used to indicate that what we are seeing is what the character is seeing – it is from their 'point of view'. Also known as 'subjective camera'.

Radio Mic A microphone without wires that can be attached to the body. It usually involves wearing a small transmitter hidden somewhere in your costume. Not widely employed because of the problems associated with unwanted noises such as rustling clothes, heartbeats and digestive processes!

Reaction Shot A shot in which the reaction of an actor to what has happened is recorded to be edited into the scene. More specific than a 'noddy'.

Reset The director is going to 'go again'. This is an instruction to prepare everything (actors, props, scenery) to re-record the same scene.

Rolling This means that the shoot is underway. You may hear 'Keep rolling', in which case the director is asking the camera to keep recording without re-marking the take with the clapperboard. It will usually be followed by the instruction 'pick it up again from the line xxx. Go.' You need to maintain your concentration during this short hiatus.

Rushes The raw, uncut material that is viewed soon after recording. It will steer the director and editor's decisions about which material to use and whether (God forbid!) the actors need to be called back to do it all again.

Special A theatrical term referring to a lighting effect for a specific purpose and not part of the general lighting state. The actor may have to ensure they are correctly positioned for this special.

Steadicam® A brand name for a camera stabilizer that enables the camera operator to follow the action without using a track by absorbing any shaking and bumping.

Story Arc This refers to a television series where a character or story carries over from one episode to another or even occurs in several episodes as part of a running plot or subplot. Such an arc presents particular challenges for an actor, who, though well acquainted with their backstory and superobjective, may have to adapt to new demands if the story arc presents them with changes to their character's history.

Supporting Actor/Artist Also still known as 'extras', Supporting Actors are employed for general or crowd scenes. They will not receive individual directions (nor credits), just generic instructions (e.g. 'Look surprised!').

Take Each recording between 'Action!' and 'Cut!'

Tracking (Shot) Unlike 'panning', tracking involves the camera moving alongside the action on a dolly that runs on a track. This ensures a smooth shot unaffected by the gait of the camera operator. It is extensively used for shooting actors walking and talking together, for example on a pavement. The actors may have to time their action to arrive at a specific point in the dialogue.

Two-Shot (TS) A shot taking in two characters. There may be others in the scene but a two-shot will involve just two of them. You may also hear 'Three-shot'.

Walk-Ons Characters employed to play non-speaking parts. They will not be part of the plot or narrative action directly and will receive minimal direction, usually from the AD.

WRAP 'It's a WRAP!' is the shout at the end of the recording process. It is usually followed by a round of applause and cheers, even though it may mean the actors are now out of work, and the intense work of the director, editor and post-production crew begins! Some believe it stands for 'wind, reel and print' or maybe that the material is ready to be wrapped up and sent to the film processors (in the days when it was). Or it may just be adapted from the common broadcasting sign-off 'That just about wraps it up!'

Genres

Drama A film or TV recording employing naturalistic acting styles. This can include fantasy and sci-fi material.

Horror This genre can employ the same naturalism as drama but, depending on the directorial style, may require a more 'heightened' portrayal of emotions and physicality.

Medical Dramas It's obvious what these are but beware: they may involve the ability to memorize accurately complex medical terms and to speak clearly at speed.

Procedural A drama genre in which a 'procedure' is involved. This includes courtroom dramas, police dramas and forensic science dramas.

Romcom (Romantic Comedy) A drama about relationships but involving misunderstandings and much humour. Almost always they have a happy ending.

Screwball Comedy A particular and sophisticated brand of comedy using both fast and witty dialogue and a slapstick approach to the acting style.

Sitcom (Situation Comedy) The humour of a sitcom lies in what we know of the characters and their relationships. The characters are consistent from episode to episode, often with a running narrative, and the humour lies in our enjoyment created by the characters' relationships in different situations.

Acting terms

Backstory You may have a great deal of information about your character from the script or even other relevant research (the 'given circumstances'). It will help you define your objectives and motivations if you are aware of these, which you can then develop into a fuller 'backstory'. Depending on the script, you may have a great deal of leeway to create this backstory, but you will also need to ensure that it fits with the needs of the film. Don't be too indulgent.

Emotion Memory A Stanislavskian term, like most in this list, emotion memory is recalling from your own life an incident when you felt the same range of emotions. This will help you identify with the character and more accurately reproduce the required actions and reactions using emotional recall. But note our health warning on page 36.

Given or Previous Circumstances Stanislavski again. Related to creating your backstory, the given circumstances are what you know, from the script (what you say, what you do, what other characters say about you), and which underpin your portrayal of the character.

If (or the '**Magic If**') Also derived from Stanislavskian theory, the 'Magic If' is a basic tool for naturalistic acting, whether for stage or screen. It consists of asking yourself the question 'if' I was this person/in this situation/at this time/wanting to achieve this objective what would I do? Engaging with these questions opens up the creative possibilities for you as an actor in exploring and making real the character.

Immediate Circumstances We have included this because there are times, especially when moving between locations and where there is also a time gap (see Chapter 8), that particular immediate events need to be recalled. You are gasping for air as your damaged spacesuit on your spacewalk gives way: cut to the safety of the airlock and you must bring the immediate circumstance with you.

Inner Monologue We do not say everything that passes through our minds (thankfully!), but what we actually say and do as a character will be the result of what is going on inside their head. As an actor you need to be aware of this inner monologue, whilst at the same time hanging on to the controlling processes of you the actor.

Motivation This is used in a slightly different way in acting theory. The actors ask themselves why they are saying what they are saying as the characters. Why does she do the actions that she does, from moving, to standing, to picking up a newspaper? In our own lives we act instinctively and we need to understand the instincts that lie behind the actions of our characters.

Objectives Your objective is what you (the character) wants to achieve. What you do or say will be aimed at achieving that objective. You might enter the kitchen with the simple objective of getting a snack and be faced by a character whose objective is to murder you. Your objective will then change to one of survival. The clashing of different objectives from different characters is the energy of the drama.

Offer An improv term meaning an action or piece of dialogue that opens the way for the response from others. In scripted material such as a film, it can include the way that the line is delivered (*see* Subtext), which opens up possibilities. Even an aggressive, stonewalling delivery of a line can be an offer, as it may give the responder a useful key to unlocking the delivery of their next line.

Physical Life How the character moves, their physical gestures, their gait, their posture. This will be related to their backstory, their class, their employment, their age and the situation in which we see the character interact with others.

Subtext We do not say all we mean and we often mean something other than the apparent import of the words we use. 'Is there any cheese in the fridge?' might actually mean 'Will you make me a sandwich?'. 'You are the most unusual person I've ever met' could mean 'You're weird' or 'You're intriguing'. It is related to inner monologue, and you will have to make decisions about the subtext of all you say.

Superobjective If 'objectives' are about the step-by-step ways we use to pursue our character's motivations, the superobjective involves standing back and looking over the trajectory of the whole course of the action. This doesn't mean playing the beginning as if you know how it all ends! The purpose of defining for yourself your superobjective is to ensure that each motivation and objective pursued has a coherence when the dénouement is played. It is about knowing the journey you are on.

Vocal Life How the character speaks, taking account of class, background, education, regional accent, health, age and the given circumstances (e.g. am I trying to impress/fit in?). It will be related to your research into your backstory.

RECOMMENDED FURTHER READING

Benedetti, J. (2005), *The Art of the Actor*, London: Methuen.
Black, D. (1990), *The Actor's Audition*, New York: Vintage.
Cannon, D. (2012), *In-Depth Acting*, London: Oberon.
Comey, J. (2002), *The Art of Film Acting*, New York: Focal Press.
Kissel, H. (2000), *Stella Adler – The Art of Acting*, London: Applause.
Meisner, S. (1987), *Sanford Meisner on Acting*, New York: Vintage Books.
Shurtleff, M. (2009), *Audition: Everything an Actor Needs to Know to Get the Part*, London: Bloomsbury.
Strasberg, L. (1988), *A Dream of Passion: The Development of the Method*, London: Penguin.

REFERENCES

Astor, M. (1997), *Playing to the Camera*, Chelsea, MI: Bookcrafter Inc.
Brown, H. J. Jr (2007), *Complete Life's Little Instruction Book*, London: Thomas Nelson Inc./Harper Collins.
Brownlow, K. (1973), *The Parade's Gone By*, London: Abacus.
Caine, M. (1997), *Acting in Film*, London: Applause.
Callery, D. (2001), *Through the Body*, London: Nick Hern.
Hayden, S. (1998), *Wanderer*, Lanham, MD: Sheridan House.
Kazan, E. (1988), *A Life*, London: Andre Deutsch.
Lee, H. (2015), *Go Set a Watchman*, London: Heinemann.
Loew, B. (2010), *Playbills to Photoplays: Stage Performers Who Pioneered the Talkies*, Bloomington, IN: Xlibris.
Lowe, V. (2007), 'Acting with Feeling: Robert Donat, the "Emotion Chart" and The Citadel (1938)', *Film History: An International Journal, 19: 73–85.*
Pearson, R. E. (1992), *Eloquent Gestures: The Transformation of Performance Style in the Griffith Biograph Films*, Berkeley: California University Press.
Richards, T. (1995), *At Work with Grotowski on Physical Actions*, London: Routledge.
Silverberg, L. (1994), *The Sanford Meisner Approach*, Lyme, NH: Smith and Kraus.
Stanislavski, C. (1949), *Building a Character*, trans. E. R. Hapgood, London: Routledge.
Stevens, J. (1997), *Actors Turned Directors*, Los Angeles: Silman James Press.

VIDEO RESOURCES

Website examples of some of the exercises can be found at: https://vimeo.com/channels/1445243.

Milton Keynes UK
Ingram Content Group UK Ltd.
UKHW020141151223
434423UK00008B/155

9 781350 093034